COMPUTERS

AND SMALL FRIES

A Computer-Readiness Guide for Parents of Tots, Toddlers and Other Minors

Mario Pagnoni

AVERY PUBLISHING GROUP INC.
Wayne, New Jersey

Cover design by Martin Hochberg and Rudy Shur
Cover layout by Martin Hochberg
Cover photo by John Edwards © 1983
Appendix photo by John Judson
Text illustrations by Tim Peterson
Cartoons by Pamela Tapia
In-house editor: Jacqueline Balla

If you would like a copy of the photograph image in poster form (18″ × 24″), please send $10.00 (includes postage and handling in U.S.) to: H.W. Rinehart Fine Arts, Inc., 245 West 75th Street, Suite 3D, New York, NY 10023.

Library of Congress Cataloging-in-Publication Data

Pagnoni, Mario
    Computers and small fries.

    Includes index.
    1. Computers and children.   I. Title.
QA76.9.C659P34   1986   649′.68   86-17442
ISBN   0-89529-350-1 (pbk.)

Printed in the United States of America

9 8 7 6 5 4 3 2 1

Contents

Acknowledgments

First, as always, I wish to thank my wife, Cammie, for her patience and cooperation as I tried to balance family life, a full-time job, and the writing of *Computers and Small Fries*.

Thanks also to my sons, James and Joseph, who patiently endured my writing sessions and helped me to review computer products.

I'd like to thank all the children at Cammie's Family Day Care Home for their warmth and humor, which I hope is reflected in the pages of this book.

I am indebted to my friends Bill Balsam, Wayne Gilgore, and Eric Eldred of the Southern New Hampshire Apple Core for their objective criticism of early drafts of the manuscript.

I am particularly grateful to Tom and Jay Spinella, who helped to design, simplify, and build the computer work station described in the Appendix.

Deep thanks also for the ideas and deft editing of the people at Avery Publishing, especially Stephen Blauer, Rudy Shur, and Jacqueline Balla.

Many thanks to Wayne Janvrin, for his assistance with Commodore software reviews, to Michael D'Arezzo, for his answers to my Atari questions, and to Jack Welch, for his answers to my Apple and IBM questions.

Finally, I am deeply grateful to Joseph R. Austin III for his technical support and advice, his cheerful good nature, and most of all, his friendship.

Preface

This book is for those parents who want to get their *pre-schoolers* started on the road to intelligent computer use. I first sensed the need for such a book while helping my school system to set up a town-wide computer-readiness course. Arbitrarily setting the lower limit for applicants at third grade, we began a modest publicity campaign. Sign-up day proved to be a revelation. Every kid on the east coast showed up! We had to move partition after partition in the open-classroomed building to accommodate all the students and their parents. During and after the session I was bombarded with questions from puzzled parents. "What about my second grader?" "And my kindergartener?" "My twins are only three, but they're very bright—when will they be ready to start computing?"

Everybody wanted to know when and how to get their kids involved in the computer revolution, what kind of computer to buy, and which software to consider. Phone calls and correspondence that I regularly received convinced me that people in other areas had the same concerns, the same questions.

This book addresses those concerns and answers those questions. It will help you to make decisions concerning the many choices facing you: when and how to start kids computing, selecting a computer and appropriate software, and other kid-friendly "extras." It will help you to make intelligent decisions about your child's computing future. I have drawn upon my experience as a parent, computer science teacher, software evaluator, and free-lance writer.

In addition, I have done extensive, informal research with the cooperation of Cammie's Family Day Care Home. Cammie is a very special day-care provider who also happens to be my wife. Having youngsters of various ages right in my own home has made it convenient for me to observe them using computers.

Thus, I have worked with children from the age of four and a half years down to fourteen months. All of this has brought me much joy, because I enjoy learning, computers, and small fries (especially the small fries).

For all the small fries at Cammie's
working themselves at the keyboard—and into my heart.

"I remember when they used to bring a football or a stuffed animal."

1

Computers and Small Fries?

All the hype about the computer being the "greatest educational tool since chalk" aside, there really *is* reason for great optimism. Computing *is* becoming easier. Software programs *are* becoming more exciting and valuable to the user every day. Younger and younger children are playing and learning at the keyboard with Mom and Dad. Indeed, children take to computers like nothing you've ever seen before. They're experts at gathering information from TV screens. My three-and-a-half-year-old friend, Raquel Bennett, pointed to an eight-sided figure and proudly declared, "Ock-A-Gon!"

"How did you know that?" I asked in disbelief.

"Well," she answered, annoyed at my ignorance, "I heard it on Ses-A-Street!"

Infants and toddlers crave stimulation, and the lively sounds and vivid images of computer programs may be just what Piaget ordered. Manipulation of computer images may help turn pre-schoolers into the active learners that the Swiss psychologist talked about. In short, computers can help stimulate your child's intellectual growth.

Toddlers and pre-schoolers using computers learn shapes, colors, upper- and lower-case letters, opposites, word recognition, pattern recognition, spelling, reading, arithmetic, reasoning skills, and hand/eye coordination. Moreover, they learn to use the computer as a tool for creative play. The key to the computer's early success is *interaction*. Children interact *with* the computer—what they do at the keyboard determines what happens on the screen, and vice-versa. Unlike the passive experience of television, computer learners must be active, responding to the computer as the computer responds to them. This imparts a sense of control to members of "the sand-box set," who too often can't reach that toy on the second shelf, or get that box of raisins opened, or do other things without a grown-up's help.

KIDS ON KEYS (SPINNAKER SOFTWARE) is an interactive keyboard familiarity program for children. As letters float down from the top of the screen, the child must locate and type the corresponding keys before the floating letters disappear from view. The program includes suitable sound effects and rewards for accurate typing. Entertaining drill programs like these encourage kids to do their otherwise dull lessons. Just watch any pre-schooler using CHARLIE BROWN'S ABCs (RANDOM HOUSE) and you'll see what I mean. Tapping a key produces a picture of an object whose name begins with the corresponding letter. Children watch with great interest as the F key produces a football and, of course, Lucy holding it for Charlie Brown to kick. Then they giggle happily as a cleverly-animated Charlie is tricked again, falling on his behind as Lucy snatches the ball away at the last minute.

Visually-appealing graphics and interesting sound effects, then, are two advantages of computer learning. Also, the computer provides immediate feedback, has infinite patience, and, as the mother of one handicapped child said, "It [the computer] has no preconceptions about my son's abilities or disabilities." Moreover, computers are consistent and objective—two qualities parents often find hard to achieve. The "father of behavioral psychology," B. F. Skinner, has said, "A good computer program can interest students in almost anything."

Many educators report great feelings of confidence built by computing tykes. Young children take great pride in being just as good as grown-ups at creating legible computer output. Even the tiniest, unskilled finger can generate neat, clear characters. Beginning writers find the monitor a welcome replacement for that troublesome paper that's always smudging and tearing. As children's motor coordination improves, they can better deal with paper and pencil. Meanwhile, they have found an easier way to express the written word. Computer-age parents who subscribe to this philosophy are quick to point out that they haven't avoided handwriting—they have merely postponed it until the children were better able to cope with it.

A major benefit of computer learning is that many programs lend themselves so well to the parent and child working together. Children can work together at the keyboard, too. A colorful, entertaining software program often makes cooperative play the order of the day. In addition, there are appropriate programs for a child working alone, at times when friends are not around or Mom and Dad are too busy.

Another benefit of computer learning is that a child's lessons can be paced and individualized. Parents can control which lesson their children will cover. Some programs are able to keep track of responses and provide either harder or simpler questions, as appropriate. Others even have record-keeping features.

Everyone knows that reading books with children is great for their vocabulary development. But a computer can be even better. After all, what other storybook is interactive and combines color, animation, and sound?

Powerful software programs like those for managing data or processing words are rapidly becoming the focal points of computer education. Does this mean that pre-schoolers are missing the boat? After all, toddlers can hardly be expected to create a database (computerized electronic file) of their toys (if they did, they could present Santa with a professional printout, sorting yuletide toy requests by name, manufacturer, type, cost, or other such Santa-helpful categories). Pre-schoolers generally don't write magazine articles or stories either (would you believe, *Recollections of a Cabbage Patch Junky?*). The point is, these are things that the child *may want to do in the near future*, and becoming familiar with the computer at an early age may just be worth it. Indeed, a child can do many of these things *with a parent* as soon as he is able to dictate his stories, data, etc. Creating and updating a database (perhaps collections of rocks, bugs, leaves, or pictures) can help children to master concepts like "numbers," "sets," "and," "or," and "not." Telling stories to a parent, who in turn types them into the computer, can nurture an early interest in creative writing. Using these programs in addition to more traditional parent-child activities will help children to master the basics, "make friends" with the computer, and accept it as just another tool—a wonderful and powerful one.

My young friend, Sean, has done some pretty interesting things with his Apple computer. He didn't start computing until the age of nine ("over the hill" in comparison to some of today's techie toddlers), but he's already retired as editor-in-chief of a computer-generated neighborhood newsletter. He hired a couple of friends as reporter and cartoonist. Together, they interviewed neighbors, wrote the copy, produced the newsletter on Sean's dot matrix printer, distributed the product for ten cents per copy, and split the profits. Now twelve years old, he recalls, "I retired young—actually, we went bankrupt—but we sure learned a lot." A lot indeed—writing skills, reporting techniques, newspaper layout, small business management— not bad for a couple of ten-year-olds. (By the way, Sean's dad, Wayne, is an avid computer hobbyist who influenced his son by his example and advice.)

Sean's home computer also helped him to win First Prize in his school's science fair. For me, a science fair project used to be a three-step task: (1) Get poster board and looseleaf paper; (2) Draw volcano on poster board; (3) Write volcano report (paraphrased from an encyclopedia) on looseleaf paper. But Sean's project was different, as are the projects of many of today's computer-savvy kids. Sean came up with an original idea. "I wonder what effect computer games have on heart rate and blood pressure?" he mused. He then set up an experiment to find out. Using a TIMEX Healthcheck Blood and Pulse Meter, he took the vital signs of people of different ages and sexes and logged the data on PFS (Personal Filing System), an easy-to-use, data-managing program. Then he gave his subjects a short instruction period and let them play an action-packed video game for five minutes. Afterwards, he retook the readings and logged the new data. Using APPLEPLOT, a program that converts raw data into professional-looking graphs, and APPLE WRITER, a sophisticated word processor, he documented all of his findings. Although it hasn't been published in a medical journal, the study is scientific and quite impressive. "Most players' pulse went down," he says, "but since blood pressure went up, the pulse and blood pressure are not dependent on each other." Summing up, he reasoned, "More tests, of a larger number of people and different types of video games, are needed to address these questions fairly."

The point of all this is that familiarizing oneself with computers at an early age might ensure their confident use in the future. Sean started at the ripe old age of nine (when Dad bought the family's Apple II Plus computer). Today's kids are being exposed to the machines even earlier. Pre-school programs that teach color and shape recognition, concentration, memorization, and sequencing serve a dual purpose. They help kids master basic skills, and they prepare them for serious and more powerful computer use later. Of course, a child is going to learn his colors and numbers whether he has a computer or not. Therefore, the bigger picture here is getting acquainted with the technology. Computers are growing and changing rapidly, even faster than your child. The specifics that are learned about computers at three or four years of age will hardly be useful when he is out in the adult workplace. But let's not worry about Harvard or the future job market when your child is three years old—let's worry about what's best for him *now*! Avoiding a phobia of advanced computer technology by introducing these things early may be just what the doctor ordered. Pre-schoolers who regularly bang out three-sentence letters to Grandma (with a little help from Mom or Dad) on children's word processors may not become adult novelists, but they aren't likely to become "computerphobiacs" either.

WHEN IS A CHILD COMPUTER-READY?

Computer-hobbyist Harry Bierce knew that his daughter, fifteen-month-old Jennifer, was computer-ready when he observed her ability to control the TV. She could turn it on and off, change channels, and adjust the volume. He bought her a toy computer that, he says, "got her interested in the keyboard." Dad already has his own computer, and he's now in the market for another—this one will be just for Jennifer.

Gregory Jarboe knew his eighteen-month-old son, Andrew, was computer-ready when the tyke dragged a chair over to Dad's Apple II computer, climbed up, and began reaching behind it for the power switch. Gregory bought the Muppet Learning Keys (an ingenious plug-in keyboard for children—see

Chapter 4), and although it was still Dad's computer, Andrew had his own, easy-to-use keyboard.

We can foster computer-readiness in children similar to the way we foster reading-readiness. Those children who regularly see their parents reading soon become interested in the written word themselves. Those who are read *to* at an early age, and who continue to read *with* their parents, usually become proficient and happy readers. Some educators speak of "surrounding children with print" as a means of cultivating their interest in reading. The computer is just another object in the adult world, like a book, telephone, washing machine, or automobile. It is extremely useful for those of us who have a need for it, and quite unnecessary for others. (When I asked students in my computer science class what they did with their home computers, one answered, "I dust it.") Children want to explore the adult world. If our home computer is useful to us, our children will see us using it, reading manuals, typing letters, playing games, managing data, and creating graphics. They'll observe our delight in the technology's simplicity—and our frustration over its complexity. Computers, therefore, will become a big part of their landscape. They're bound to notice it, become interested and involved. After all, they're surrounded by computer technology.

If you are already using computers, your children are becoming computer-ready. You have begun the process of surrounding them with technology. If you are not using computers, maybe it's time you started. You don't have to become an expert. You don't need to use powerful and complicated programs. Some pre-school programs don't even require a manual—you can master them in no time. Computers can also be great fun. Exciting programs like THE PRINT SHOP (BRODERBUND) and MASK PARADE (SPRINGBOARD) are making a big splash nowadays. With the help of a printer, THE PRINT SHOP lets you create your own personalized greeting cards, signs, stationery, and banners. It is incredibly easy to use, and a young child placed strategically on a helpful adult's lap can create a special remembrance for a special someone. MASK PARADE provides a simple and delightful way to create masks, badges, hats, and other items. An adult can lend a hand with the program and the scissors (you actually cut out the items, decorate them, and *wear* them).

When considering children's computer-readiness, mental and motor development are bigger factors than age. Unrestricted access to an old typewriter will help you both gauge your children's computer-readiness and foster it. Are they interested in the typewriter? Do they immediately demolish the inner mechanisms, or do they treat the machine with reasonable care?

Very young children often have trouble striking just one key at a time, having the tendency to push a half dozen keys at once with the flat of the hand. Sarah (twenty months old) found great joy in this, so I let her revel in it. Gradually, she got the knack of gently tapping one key at a time, but often she still depresses the space bar accidentally while reaching for a key above it. This poses an occasional problem (striking the space bar causes several of our programs to start from the beginning). Sarah and I sometimes have trouble getting past "square one."

Letting a toddler sit on your lap and press the keys (this is the true origin of the world "keypunch") is another way to help develop computer-readiness. Computer keyboards contain a wealth of inviting buttons to push, press, poke, peck at, and otherwise mash, maul, or manhandle. You'd certainly allow a small fry to bang away on a piano keyboard. Let him have a go at the typewriter or computer keyboard as well. Scribbling and doodling via a computer screen can help children develop our conventional left to right orientation for reading. Some parents affix brightly-colored stickers to "special" keys, such as the letters of the child's first name.

Children who can associate pictures and objects with their names, turn the pages of a book one at a time, enjoy a book's pictures without munching them, switch dials on televisions and radios, and stack blocks with occasional success, can begin computing. Children who can't yet do these things are probably not computer-ready and simply need time to grow. You can help by showing them more pictures, helping them to turn more book pages and stack more blocks—in other words, by continuing to share more interesting experiences with them.

I am continually amazed at how well toddlers and pre-schoolers take to computers. Even the youngest can benefit, if only because they are sharing another part of the adult world with you.

When I began my work with children at Cammie's Family Day Care Home, I thought that the toddlers would tire after ten to fifteen minutes at the computer, and the pre-schoolers after twenty. I was wrong. The "older" kids often stayed interested for an hour or more, the "under twos" for nearly a half-hour. Occasionally, parents had to drag their children away from the keyboard, amidst the weeping and gnashing of teeth (or gums). Once, my son Joseph came into our computer room to tell Raquel that her mom had arrived and it was time to leave. Working intently at the computer, and annoyed at the interruption, Raquel said, "Tell *her* to come *here!*"

Initially, I worked with the children on an individual basis. Later the children cooperated (sort of) at the keyboard. The week before beginning the project, we "briefed" the parents and children. We would work/play at the computer for as long as the child remained interested. Computer time would be after the children's afternoon nap, while we waited for parents to come to take them home. We would use a variety of software and various computer devices.

The parents, most of whom did not have computers at home, were delighted that their children would be getting this "head start." But the children were unimpressed, or so we thought. Four-year-old Bethy was the first to, as the kids say, "do computer." After completing her first session, I brought her back to the play area and she began to tell her mom about her first computing experience. The other kids gathered around in silence and listened intently. They dropped their toys and books—some even stopped talking in mid-sentence, listening to Bethy's first-hand report. It was the E. F. Hutton of the day-care set talking. From then on, the first thing the children asked when they arrived in the morning was, "Whose turn is it to do computer today?" And whenever I appeared, their eyes lit up with expectation—who would be the lucky one to do computer today with Paggy? (That's me.)

DEVELOPMENTAL STAGES TO LOOK FOR

Children go through several stages in their exposure to computers. The first major breakthrough occurs when they understand the cause and effect of their computer input—i.e., I touch this thing and something happens on the screen; I touch this other thing and something else happens. Positioning the screen as close to the keyboard as possible can help children to make the connection between their input and the screen's output. Before making this connection, however, they usually don't do much more than slobber over the keyboard. This is to be avoided as much as possible, since slobbering and electricity don't mix.

Two and a half-year-old Diana made the connection her very first time on the computer. "What's that on the screen?" I asked her. "I don't know," she answered. Then, pointing to a key, she said, "I pushed this and it came on."

Little Matthew understood the connection between his input and the screen's output quite well—or so I thought. One afternoon I showed him how to do some computer art, using a program called KINDER COMP (SPINNAKER). Matthew, a bright four-year-old, handled the joystick like a pro. (A joystick is a small computer input device with a lever that you control a la PACMAN.) Matthew pushed the lever in all directions, drawing on our color screen. He changed the color of his "pen" by pressing one of two joystick buttons. Once he got the hang of it, Matty was able to draw all kinds of wonderful objects. At one point he created a perfect rectangle—no small feat for a novice computer-using four-year-old. "Let me show you something, Matty," I said, taking the joystick from him. I maneuvered the point of the joystick's "pen" inside the rectangle and pressed the letter F on the keyboard. The rectangle quickly became filled with a beautiful shade of red, and Matthew was suitably impressed. "*Wow*! How'd ya do that, Paggy?" he asked. "F, for Fill," I told him. Incredulous, he pointed to the computer and, looking me straight in the eye, said, "It *heard* you?"

The second stage occurs when the child can use the keyboard. Sarah tells her mom regularly, "Today is my turn to do computer with Paggy. It's easy. I just punch the buttons." Before they can operate the keyboard, however, children can use various "keyboard alternatives" (joysticks and other devices—see Chapter 4). Many of these alternatives require *some* use of the keyboard, and this leads to keyboard familiarity. With a little practice, keyboarding skill improves rapidly. Thus, one day, Bethy would search the keyboard diligently and ask, "Don't you have any W's on this thing?" A short time later she'd tell me, "I'll help you find that letter. See where my finger's pointing—press it!"

Matthew's first keyboarding experience was with another KINDER COMP program (many software packages have several games/learning activities on one disk). With this particular program, any key that is struck produces a row of that letter across the screen. Mat created his name with rows of Ms, As, and Ts. He liked what he had done, but said, "I have more room."

"Go ahead and type some more," I offered.

"I don't know what to write."

"Type anything you want. You could make Matthew," I suggested.

"Nah," he said.

"You could write Matty."

"Yeh! Yeh! How do I do that?"

"Well, you need another T and a Y." Mat shook his head in dismay as he searched the keyboard.

"What's wrong, Matty?" I asked.

"There's no T," he declared.

"Sure there is," I assured him, "you found it before." But pointing to the keyboard letter T, he said, "I already used *that* one!"

The third stage occurs when children can recognize familiar icons on the screen and respond to them appropriately. Icons are graphic messages that don't need written words to convey their meaning (like the wordless "No Smoking" signs in public buildings that show a burning cigarette with an "X" through it).

The fourth stage occurs when children's reading skills develop enough to sound out on-screen commands. Emily, a four-year-old whose parents regularly read with and to her, enjoys the TINK! TONK! software series (MINDSCAPE). These are story books on disk that require the user to choose options for the main characters. They feature music and clever graphics, and are a delight. They remind me of the *Choose Your Own Ending* book series that so enthralled my own children. Emily studies the screen choices intently—i.e., G to GO ON, S to STOP. She sounds out the letters carefully and deciphers many of the words. Then she asks, "What does GO ON mean?"

The fifth stage occurs when the child can be trusted to insert a disk, turn on the machine, and take care of it properly. CAUTION: Some children want to do all of this before they are really ready.

Finally, the last stage occurs when the adult can be trusted not to interfere with the child's own use of the computer.

For many, the key to understanding the computer and its operation lies in mastering its terminology. You might think that all the complicated-sounding jargon is incomprehensible to the average person. After all, it probably originated from computer nerds from prestigious universities. Well, I have news for you. While it is true that computerese can sound very complicated and become intimidating—the domain of adults—my research indicates that computerese actually evolved from babytalk. An appreciation of each term's origin and precise definition can often illuminate matters. To that end, we present:

Computer Baby-Babble

Access time. The amount of time Baby cries before getting attention.

Accumulator. A diaper designed for heavy-duty use.

Array. A cry of great joy, as in, "Array! My bubbie is here!"

Artificial Intelligence. What all new parents think their kids are born with.

Assembler. What Dad becomes every Christmas.

Back-up. What Baby learning to walk gets every time he falls.

Bit. What Baby did with first tooth (there are usually 8 bits to a good byte).

Boot. Short for bootie.

Buffer. What parent does to daughter after applying baby powder to her bottom.

Byte. The basic unit in feeding Baby (half a byte is termed a nibble); also, the nursing mother's greatest fear.

Call. Ma ma!—also, Da da!

CPU. A child's game of hide and seek.

Crash. What happens when Baby learns to climb.

Cursor. The parent who gets up every hour and attends to Baby while spouse feigns sleep.

Data. Pronounced Da Da; Baby's first reference to father.

Database. Dad's position in baseball.

Debug. De thing de baby gets from de dog.

Dedicated. Reserved for one child. Any kid will tell you that all his toys are dedicated and cannot be shared.

Digits. What parents count before leaving maternity ward.

Down time. The length of Baby's nap.

Global search. What takes place when frenzied parents misplace baby carriage in supermarket.

Graphics. Drawings; works of art made in many colors with various writing implements. Baby is artist—wall is canvas.

Hard disk. Zwieback cookie.

Hardware. Clothes built to last (Osh Kosh B'Gosh).

Hertz. What happens when teething begins.

High-level language. What develops when parents begin to spell out messages in presence of Baby.

IBM. Baby's happy pronouncement when finally toilet-trained.

If . . . Then. If you can make it through the first year, then the problems begin.

Information retrieval. Trying to get Baby to tell you if he swallowed those marbles.

Initialize. What you do to Baby's belongings before sending him to day care.

Input. Food; also, to put in (babies are known to input food, foreign objects, balloons, etc. into ears, nose, and other suitable orifices).

Input device. Baby's hands.

Input/Output. What happens when parent tries to feed stubborn baby.

Interface. Where babies under two put *everything*.

Internal storage. Where those marbles probably are.

Joystick. Baby's first piece of chewing gum.

Keyboard. Part of computer covered with peanut butter.

Keypunch. The way Baby strikes the computer keyboard.

Load. Contents of dirty diaper.

Mainframe. Baby who has his father's "big bones."

Memory. Kept in baby books.

Monitor. What smart parents do whenever Baby is quiet for more than two minutes.

Nano. Baby's grandfather.

Nanosecond. Baby's grandfather by another marriage.

Number crunching. When Baby eats bingo card.

Off-line. Baby asleep.

On-line. Baby awake.

Peek. A quick diaper check.

Poke. A quick diaper check; nighttime version.

Prompt. When Baby wants diaper change.

Run. What parents relearn after Baby learns to walk.

Software. Any fabric designed to touch Baby's skin; blankets, diapers.

Software package. Baby wrapped in blanket.

Statement. Baby's first word; also, the press release that follows.

Synchronous. Twins! (and they're *both* awake).

Visual display. Baby's smile; often caused by gas.

Voice output. A loud night-time cry calling for your spouse to respond. *See also* Cursor.

"Why, any young child could master this model in no time."

2

Selecting a Kid-Friendly Computer

Before you start browsing in computer stores and chatting with salespeople, you need a rudimentary understanding of some computer terms and principles. This will make you a better consumer. If you have no computer knowledge, you can disregard most of the talk about *compilers* and *hard disks*, and *megahertz* of this and *megabyte* of that. In the following section, I've focused on those terms that are most helpful for novices. Of course, you may want to pick up a computer book for explanations of other jargon. There are many to choose from. Some are even helpful, like Michael Crichton's *Electronic Life* and Peter McWilliams' *The Personal Computer Book*.

If computer books intimidate you, try reading some that are geared for children. Authors of kids' books do what all authors should do—they try to explain things clearly. (And if somebody catches you reading them, you can always say you bought them as gifts for your kids.)

PRE-SHOPPING COMPUTERESE

Salespeople will often bandy the term *user-friendly* about. If something is user-friendly, it's supposed to be easy to learn and easy to use. Believe it when you see it.

Hardware refers to the computer itself and such components as computer screens and printers. The computer is often called a *CPU*, or *Central Processing Unit*.

Components other than the main computer are referred to as *peripherals*. They're attached on the periphery, or outside the main unit; printers, keyboard alternatives, etc.

Software refers to all those overpriced disks in fancy packages that you see all over computer stores. They're the programs that tell the computer how to do its stuff. Software is to computers what records are to stereos.

Floppy disk

Disk drives are the devices into which you place all those overpriced disks. The drives "read" the disks and display the programs on your screen.

Floppy disk drive

An *interface* is the connecting link between a computer component and the main computer. Salespeople are fond of using this as a verb, as in "For only $600 you can interface your computer to this stupendous printer." Beware—those hungry young salespeople are adept at interfacing with your wallet!

A *port* is a socket where peripherals get plugged in.

A *printer* is an important peripheral that allows you to print out your computer work. It is a kind of automatic typewriter without keys. Through your computer, you send your printer a message to start printing, then go about your business.

Printer

The *keyboard* is the part of the computer through which the user inputs his instructions. It is very much like a typewriter keyboard with a few additional keys. These additional keys appear confusing, but actually make things easier for the user.

Keyboard

A *CRT (Cathode Ray Tube)* is a monitor—the computer screen. Monitors are often *monochrome*; that is, one color (usually white, green, or amber on a black or green background). Most pre-school software programs make use of color. A *color monitor*, then, is a must.

Monitor

Pixels are points of light. The word itself is derived from "picture element." A monitor that displays many pixels produces a clear, sharp image. The more pixels there are, the better.

Resolution refers to the clarity of screen images. *High resolution* means there are many pixels per unit of screen. Salespeople talk of letters and numerals being clearly *resolved*. Since quality means big bucks, be sure to clearly resolve how you are going to pay for it.

A *menu* is a program's list of options from which the user can choose. Programs that proceed from one menu to another are often considered user-friendly and are termed *menu-driven*.

Terms like *64K* or *128K* refer to how much *memory* a computer has. The more memory available, the more sophisticated the software can be. In addition to finding the software you want and determining which brand of computer runs it, be sure the model you choose has enough memory to support it. Good software packages clearly label the program's hardware requirements.

Documentation is a fancy name for the manuals that accompany the computer and software. Most used to be atrocious. They are getting better all the time. As author William Zinsser has said so aptly, "If any single force is destined to impede man's mastery of the computer, it will be the manual that tries to teach him to master it." Examine the manuals that come with the hardware you are considering. Are they readable? With a little confidence in yourself and coherent documentation, you *can* master this machine!

FINDING THE RIGHT COMPUTER

Finding the right computer is easy. First, determine what you want to do with it (write novels, run a small business, teach pre-schoolers to read and write). Next, find the appropriate software programs (see Chapter 7) and, finally, purchase the machine that runs that software. Keeping toddlers and pre-schoolers in mind, you should also consider which machines are compatible with important "keyboard alternatives," such as light pens and Muppet Learning Keys (see below). Keyboard alternatives are computer input devices that can be used *instead of*, or in conjunction with, the keyboard. They can make "communicating" with computers easier. One obvious advantage of circumventing the traditional keyboard is that the user needn't know how to type. More importantly, in the case of young children, they *don't have to know how to read*. And in some instances, as with a light pen, they don't even need to know the letters of the alphabet.

A light pen is a kind of stylus that is connected to the computer by a thin cable. It allows the user to write, draw, or scribble directly onto the computer screen. This is the same device that NFL sportscasters use to graphically recap football plays.

Muppet Learning Keys is the first input device designed especially for children. An ingenious 14″ × 15″ keyboard, it can be placed right on the child's lap, and is plugged into the computer game port. Its extra large and logically arranged keys (letters are ordered alphabetically) make it easy for tiny fingers to explore numbers, letters, colors, and punctuation marks. (Keyboard alternatives are described in detail in Chapter 4.)

When you consider buying a computer, determine how much software is available for it and, specifically, how much of it is targeted for pre-schoolers. Software is *machine specific*; that is, it runs on one specific machine. You can't buy an Apple Computer software program and bring it home to use on your Commodore. Fortunately, the better software packages feature versions for several different computers. For example, there is a version of the MASK PARADE program mentioned in Chapter 1 for Apple and IBM computers. When you see a program you like, take note which machines run it. Keep in mind that a software manufacturer who creates a popular program that runs on just one type of computer is likely to release versions for other computers in the future. A phone call to the software vendor could confirm this.

Consider the Learning Language, LOGO

Some computer languages are built into computers. BASIC is the most commonly built-in language. Other languages are stored on disks and must be loaded into the computer's memory each time you want to use them. LOGO is one such language. Although today's programming language skills may change drastically in the future, the knowledge gained from *learning how to learn* may last forever. From this perspective, LOGO is the best language to introduce to your children. Seymour Papert, the renowned M.I.T. professor and author of *Mindstorms*, says, ". . . In my vision, the child programs the computer and, in so doing, both acquires a sense of mastery over a piece of the most modern and powerful technology and establishes an intimate contact with some of the deepest ideas from science, from mathematics, and from the art of intellectual model building." In his introduction to *Mindstorms*, Papert writes that the book ". . . is about using computers to challenge current beliefs about who can understand what and at what age." LOGO, his brainchild, is a wonderful learning tool. Be sure to purchase a machine that runs it. Most of today's top-selling computers run some version of LOGO. (See Chapter 7 for a capsule review of KINDERLOGO, a pre-school version of LOGO.)

A Kid's Computer—Basic Requirements

Look for a computer that supports floppy disk drives. These, you will recall, are devices that "read" the disks upon which your programs are written. They can "write" on disks, too, giving you *external storage*. The same thing can be done with cassette players and tapes, but tapes are very slow, error-prone, and tedious to work with. Two disk drives are better than one for saving data and making back-up copies of programs. One floppy disk drive, however, will suffice. You *do not* need a *hard disk drive*, which is for increased data storage and serious business applications.

Your computer should be expandable. Can you add more memory later on? Does the machine support popular keyboard alternatives? Will the machine be able to grow along with your family and its needs? It should also have a typewriter-like keyboard. Even if, for now, you decide to by-pass the keyboard, you will eventually need it. A standard keyboard arrangement is advisable.

Your computer should be compatible with a good printer. Once children begin to generate stories and art work, they'll want to print out copies for friends and relatives. A *dot matrix* printer is usually cheaper than a *letter quality* one. Letter quality means clear, readable printouts. While dot matrix printouts are readable, they are not quite up to letter quality. On the other hand, many letter quality printers won't do graphics printouts, and many dot matrix printers can. Exciting programs like MASK PARADE and THE PRINT SHOP, mentioned in Chapter 1, require *certain* dot matrix printers.

A child's computer must output to a color monitor—most pre-school software programs make use of color graphics. It doesn't make much sense to buy a program that teaches colors if you only have access to a black and white screen. Some adult programs also rely on color for their effectiveness. The electronic version of SCRABBLE, though not nearly as entertaining as the swivel-board version, comes in handy when there are no human opponents around. But it is difficult to play on a monochrome screen. It's hard to distinguish between "double word score" and "triple letter score" spaces on the board. And, as any kid will tell you, FROGGER is a real bummer without color—you can't tell if you're over a lily pad or under an automobile.

WARNING: Color monitors produce more radiation than monochrome models. Of course, there is disagreement concerning exactly how harmful television and monitor radiation can be. See Chapter 6 for more information on computers and radiation.

There are several ways to get color output. You can purchase a *composite* monitor. This is essentially a color TV that is unable to receive television signals. It has been modified for better color and sharper images. (Some composite monitors double as color televisions.) Or you might purchase an *RGB* (Red, Green, Blue) monitor. RGBs produce very sharp images and very clearly-defined color. RGBs often need special plug-in computer cards (interfaces). CAUTION: Some computers just can't accommodate RGB monitors. You can also purchase a combination composite and RGB monitor. But the cheapest way out is probably to buy an adapter called an *RF Modulator*. Such a device lets you interface with a color television that you may already have. The images may not be crystal clear, but they are more than adequate for games and pre-school programs. Many hobbyists buy a device allowing them to switch back and forth between a color TV and a monochrome monitor. They use one when they need color, the other when they need clearer resolution. Whichever monitor you choose, check it out while it is hooked up to the computer you plan to buy.

Look for a computer whose manufacturer has had enough computer sales to make the production of software by independent vendors profitable. Also, the manufacturer should be stable enough financially to indicate its ability to provide continued customer support.

Finally, consider your own personal economics. Some computer hobbyists advise you to buy the least expensive model possible and see if the kids use it. Paying several thousand dollars for a computer might result in (a) an expensive dust collector, or (b) children who are pressured into using the machine so that their parents "get their money's worth." (Shades of, "We paid two grand for that piano—now *go practice!*")

Some Computer-hunting Do's and Don'ts

Do look for a good dealer before you look for a good deal. "My dealer was very helpful *in selling me the machine*," lamented one new computer owner. Such a complaint is all too common.

Hobbyists get a great price, later experience problems, and then get little or no dealer service or support. "More than buying a computer, you are buying *a place to buy a computer*," cautioned one savvy consumer.

Do try out machines in libraries, computer stores, and friends' homes.

Do look for durability. While not meant to be dribbled like a basketball, a computer should be able to take the ordinary pounding of children's fingers (unless, as one computer manual says, you type with a hammer).

Do bring the family to try out the machine. Common sense will often determine if a feature is appropriate for children. For example, some computers have an "auto-repeat" feature, which causes a key that is touched and held down to repeat. This can present a problem for children, who cannot seem to get their fingers off the keys soon enough.

Do look at software as carefully as you examine hardware. Software is the vital link in successful computing. Look at lots of it. After a while, you will get a feel for what is mediocre and what is innovative and valuable.

Do look for a manufacturer without a history of releasing incompatible upgrades of its previous computers. Stated simply, newer models of the same brand of computer should be able to run the older model's software. That way, if you buy an upgraded model in the future, your entire software library will not be obsolete.

Do ask the dealer these questions: If the computer is broken, who's going to fix it? How long is this likely to take? Will there be a minimum charge? On-site service is a big plus.

Do consider what kinds of computers the local schools will be using. You may want the same computer for your home.

Don't take computer courses, at least not at the beginning, unless you know that the instructor can clearly convey computer information to novices. Most computer instructors are beauties. They spew out terms like *hexadecimals* and *sequential files*. They seem to relish the fact that they understand something that we don't. Most "computer types" have absolutely no idea just how bewildering all of this can be to the rest of us. If you are a confirmed course-taker, look for the increasingly popular "parent and child" classes.

Don't underestimate the importance of good manuals. Are they readable? CAUTION: You may discover, as I did, that most manuals are written by the same guys who teach those computer courses!

Don't give up on a manual just because *all* is not clear upon first reading. Mastering new material requires some effort on your part. User-friendliness is an art, not yet a science. With a little confidence in yourself and readable manuals, you can master the machine. Then you can help the small fries in your life to do the same.

In the final analysis, many popular computers are suitable for pre-schoolers. And the more popular sellers have a great deal of adult software available in case you're considering using the machine as a family tool. Computing parents are split on this issue—some believe in the *family computer*, and say in effect, "Why buy a second computer? The kids will learn to use ours by observing and working/playing with us. They won't ruin it because we'll be right beside them." Others think that kids should have their own inexpensive "starter computer."

Stephen and Sheryl, computer consultants from Indiana, believe that children should have their own computers. After buying one for their children, Emily, age three, and Reuben, age one, they decided not to use it for their own personal use. It would belong to Emily and Reuben. "We wouldn't put the house budget or word processing on it," said Stephen, "so it would be available for them when they were ready to use it."

COMPUTER CLUBS/USERS' GROUPS

Locating a computer club is really the first step in your journey toward becoming a competent computer-user. Visit your local computer store and ask about the locations of users' groups. Computer dealers are usually happy to give customers such information. Other good leads are computer repair/service shops and college or high school computer departments. And even in this age of "accessing electronic databases," the best resource in America is often a friendly librarian. If all else fails, write to the computer manufacturer. Once you locate the group, it's a good idea to attend computer club meetings even before buying a computer. Drop in on a few monthly meetings, get acquainted, ask questions. While there are bound to be some "nerds" and "propeller-heads" in the crowd, you'll find kindred spirits too. And who says a nerd can't be a kindred spirit? The meetings are generally informal, with no one after you for dues until you decide to become a "regular." Computer hobbyists are often "upgrading" their hardware, so you might find a bargain on a good, used machine. These upgrading hobbyists might even "throw in" software that they no longer need.

Computer clubs have lots of advantages, including: regular meetings featuring guest speakers and demonstrations of new products, a newsletter, group purchase deals, and public domain software (a library of computer software written by club members or donated by affiliate club members who choose to make them available to the public). A club librarian organizes and maintains the software, making copies for members (usually for a nominal fee) upon request.

In addition, user groups feature *Special Interest Groups (SIGs)*. These subgroups, often the lifeblood of the club, zero in on people's interests. *SIGs* for education (*EDSIG*) and beginners (*BIG*) are often very popular. Perhaps you'll even find a *PIG* (pre-schoolers' interest group).

Finally, you'll get answers to your many questions. Indeed, the best thing you can probably get from a club is support. Often, the local computer club is the *only* place that offers the kind of support that novice computer-users need. Computer dealers haven't been able to deliver that support so far; neither have manufacturers' 800 telephone numbers and hotlines. As one club member put it, "Most salespeople and technicians know just enough to sell the computer. Our club is the answer to that problem, and to all those atrocious computer manuals."

MAJOR COMPUTERS RECOMMENDED FOR USE WITH CHILDREN

The popular pre-school programs reviewed in Chapter 7 run on either Apple, Atari, Commodore, or IBM computers (the software manufacturer often makes versions that run on several of these machines). Therefore, I've included some specifics regarding these computers. When price-shopping, remember to consider the same components: computer, disk drive, color monitor, and optional peripherals (printers, joysticks, light pens, etc.) so that you will know exactly what you are getting for your money.

Monitor, Keyboard, Disk drive and Printer

Apple

You should consider both the Apple IIe and the Apple IIc. Both are general purpose machines that can run an incredible number of educational software packages. Most Apple software runs on both the IIe and the IIc, as well as the older Apple II Plus (which, by the way, makes a good children's computer, and can be picked up pretty cheaply from upgrading hobbyists). The IIe comes standard with 64K and can be easily upgraded to 128K, while the IIc comes standard with 128K. Since both the IIe and IIc generally come with monochrome monitors, you will have to pay extra for a color monitor. Both computers feature standard typewriter-style keyboards. And while both offer good color graphics, their sound capabilities are limited.

The IIc is a more compact version of the IIe. It comes with a built-in disk drive (a disadvantage of this is that when your disk drive is off to the repair shop, so is your computer). The IIe is more expandable, with eight expansion slots under the lid. The IIc, on the other hand, has a sealed lid allowing for expansion only through its ports at the back of the machine. This may be an advantage with pre-schoolers, however, since it prevents tinkering inside the circuitry.

Other differences include the fact that the IIc produces either 40 or 80 columns (40 or 80 characters across the screen), while the IIe produces 40 (unless expanded to 80). The larger characters of a forty-column screen may be better for pre-schoolers.

At the time of this writing, Apple's Macintosh, though a fine machine for the home or small business, appears unsuitable for use with pre-schoolers. This is because it supports neither a reasonably-priced color monitor nor a significant volume of pre-school software.

Another choice definitely worth considering is the newer Apple II GS. It does what the other Apples do—and more. (Apple engineers have placed the entire Apple IIe computer on one chip in the GS.) The GS stands for Graphics, Sound (and Speed), and the machine is nearly three times faster than the IIe and delivers remarkable sound and graphics. Combining the best features of all the Apple computers, the GS is very expandable, runs most of the wide base of Apple II software, and comes with mouse, detachable keyboard, numeric keypad, and 256K of memory.

For more information, write Apple Computer, Inc., 20525 Mariani Ave., Cupertino, CA 95014.

Commodore

You should consider both the Commodore 64 and the newer, more powerful Commodore 128. Commodore doesn't have the amount of software that Apple does, but there are many good programs and a less expensive price tag. Commodore computers feature terrific graphic and sound capabilities for pre-schoolers. They feature a voice synthesizer chip called SID (Sound Interface Device), which accounts for the great sound. Software that helps the user to create music takes full advantage of this chip. The C64 disk drive is slow. Another consideration is that cartridge software is available for some of Commodore's pre-school programs, which may be easier for small fries to use.

The Commodore 128 expands the C64 keyboard and adds a numeric keypad, 40 or 80 column display (with Commodore's RGB monitor), and a new and faster disk drive. It runs all C64 programs, programs written especially for the 128, as well as thousands of programs (some sophisticated business packages) requiring the operating system known as CP/M.

For more information, write Commodore Business Machines, 1200 Wilson Dr., West Chester, PA 19380.

Atari

Consider Atari's 800, 1200, and 1600 XL series of computers. Atari has continued to produce highly reliable, general purpose machines featuring a sizable base of software, including the pre-school packages outlined in Chapter 7.

In addition, the latest Atari upgrades to consider are the 520ST and the 1040 ST.

The 520ST features 512K and excellent sound and graphics, including a high-resolution screen display like Apple's Macintosh (but the 520ST works with a color monitor). It has a calculator-style keypad and also comes with LOGO (on disk) included in the purchase price. The 1040ST is an even more powerful version of the 520ST. These powerful machines, however, run very little software. They run the newer, 3½-inch disks rather than the more common, 5¼-inch disks. I know of no pre-school software that supports this new format.

For more information, write Atari, Inc., 1265 Borregas Ave., Sunnyvale, CA 94086.

IBM

Consider the IBM PC, as well as the discontinued IBM PCjr. Both feature good sound and color, as well as a wide base of software for adults and children. The less expensive PCjr has a 62-key detachable keyboard (with optional cordless keyboard, which uses infrared like a TV remote control). It comes with one built-in drive, and another can be attached externally. An IBM PC or a 128K PCjr may be ideal for parents who use an

IBM PC at the office. They can bring some work home to complete—if they can get the kids off the machine. A drawback to the discontinued PCjr is that service and support for the machine may be difficult to obtain in the future.

For more information, write IBM Personal Computers, P.O. Box 1328, Boca Raton, FL 33432.

3

Choosing Kid-Friendly Software

Identifying and selecting quality software can be easy if you follow several basic rules. The more software you examine, the more finely tuned your ability to evaluate it will become.

SOME BASIC GUIDELINES

It is best to trade with dealers who will let you try out programs before you purchase them. Many programs have several activities/games on a single disk. Be advised that often, there are only one or two good ones, the rest being simply "fillers."

Read magazine reviews. The authors are often computer hobbyists, educators, and/or parents who have tried out the programs with their children (be careful, though—some reviewers seem to know more about computers than they do about kids!). *Family Computing* (P.O. Box 2512, Boulder, CO 80321) has a light, readable style, and others geared toward education, like *Classroom Computer Learning* (5615 W. Cermak Road, Cicero, IL 60650) often have reviews and articles concerning very young children.

Talk with parents who have had experience with pre-school software. This is one of the primary advantages of a computer club. Also, visit local libraries and ask about software. Many libraries have computers and software for their patrons to use.

Closely examine the manufacturer's policies for replacing defective software and allowing users to make back-up copies.

A 90-day warranty on disks is desirable. Also, you should be able to get a replacement copy for a nominal fee if the disk fails beyond the 90-day period.

Many schools have at least one teacher who is familiar with computers. It may be worth telephoning the local elementary schools and speaking with the resident computer coordinators. They may offer good advice.

SPECIFICS TO CONSIDER

When you evaluate software, it is important to consider a variety of specific matters. You may find it helpful to ask the questions discussed below.

- **What are the hardware requirements of the program?** That is, what machines run it, how much memory does it need, and which input devices does it require? If the program generates printouts, which printers does it support? You may create a masterpiece on your computer screen, but if the program isn't compatible with your printer, you will be unable to print it.

- **How interactive is the software?** Interactive software requires the child to respond to the computer and vice-versa. Too much of today's software makes our children merely spectators. Is the level of interaction appropriate for your child's ability? A two-year-old may be able to make only single keystroke responses, while an older child may be able to handle several keystrokes. Good pre-school software is interactive without requiring great manual dexterity or quick reflexes. Also, computer responses to the child's input should be immediate.

- **Does the program make use of visually-appealing graphics?** Familiar characters like the Muppets and the Peanuts gang are safe bets and animation is a well-known hit. Are the graphics appropriate for a child? One alphabet program uses a picture of a Bomb for a "B" word and a Pirate with a knife in his mouth for a "P" word. A program that's designed to teach pre-schoolers the alphabet through graphics should use pictures of common objects with common names.

Umbrella is preferable to Unicycle or Ukulele, Pig better than Prism. Though this may seem like a matter of personal preference, I know from experience that Pig is in, Prism out with pre-schoolers. One child I know stared blankly at a computer picture of the "P" word—Prism. It just wasn't in her frame of reference. But when another program used the more familiar Pig, the child became excited. "Piggy! Piggy!" she shouted. "That's a fat pig." Then, collecting herself, she leaned toward me and whispered seriously, "You know what? My daddy called my mommy that last night."

Look for *hi-res (high-resolution) graphics*. These are easily distinguished from *low-res graphics* by their increased detail. My friend Matthew squinted curiously at a low-res picture trying to decide which animal it represented. He guessed Dog, Kangaroo, even Rhinoceros. When I hinted that the animal's name began with the letter B, he offered Buffalo. I finally had to tell him that it was a Bear. He shook his head skeptically and declared, "I don't know that's a bear."

Similarly, when I told Raquel that she was looking at a picture of a Horse (a very poor, low-res picture), she said correctly, "Yeh—it look like a Dragon, though." Finally, when Bethy identified a supposedly ferocious Lion as a Donut, I knew the program was in trouble.

Hi-res graphics leave no doubt as to the artist's intention, like when Devony and I admired a nicely-sketched kitten. "He's cute, isn't he?" I commented. "Paggy," corrected four-year-old Devony, "she's a *girl*—can't you see those long whiskers?"

- **Can you by-pass the *boot graphics* with a keystroke?** Boot graphics are the often elaborate introduction/demonstration/credits. Kids get impatient waiting for the action to begin. Good program design allows you to skip this introduction with the touch of a key. Similarly, a program with several activities on the same disk should allow you to easily jump from one to another without having to start the program over from the beginning.

- **Are there entertaining sound effects?** This is especially important for the youngest children. Little Jonathan's (the "baby" of the group at the age of fourteen months) eyes light up when he hears music emanating from the computer. He then proceeds to touch every key within reach, as he attempts to create a symphony. Another consideration is whether you can turn the sound off when you want quiet. Many programs prompt you with, "Do you want music? Y/N." Once, Bethy asked me, "What do I press for music?" "Y," I answered. "Because I *like* music!" she returned, indignantly.

- **Are there different levels of difficulty?** Can children of different ages/abilities use the program? This extends the "life-span" of a program considerably as the child is able to use various parts of the program as he grows older. Can the pace be increased or decreased to account for ability differences in children? Does the program track your progress and give you problems of increasing difficulty, or are you locked in to the same level? EARLY GAMES (SPRING-BOARD) features several programs that "become more difficult as they are played with success."

  Is the material appropriate for your child? You should pay only modest attention to "Suggested Ages" listed on the package. Some programs claim to be appropriate for children "three and up," or from "four to twelve." It is hard to imagine any program that both a four-year-old and a twelve-year-old would enjoy.

  I worked with Diana on a "Connect the Dots" program designed to teach alphabetical order. Proper dot connecting produced a picture of an animal. I don't think Diana was quite ready for alphabetical dot-to-dots because I had to help out quite a bit, and when I asked her, "What are we making?" she answered, "I don't know . . . maybe pimples."

  Also, before loading a program that was designed to teach beginning spelling, I asked Diana right up front, "Can you spell?" "I can spell D," she answered proudly.

  If a pre-reading program starts off with "Hi—type in your full name," you can safely assume that the program is a bit off the mark. In addition to the suitability of subject matter, you should consider the overall suitability of the software in terms of any violent, racist, sexist, or stereotypical messages that may be evident.

- **Is there an *editor mode*?** An editor mode is a program option that allows users to input their own data (spelling words, math problems, etc.). The program games can then be played with the user's own questions or data. This feature gives a program increased "staying power." Although I haven't seen editor features on pre-school software, those designed for older children can be used to make the program more appropriate for pre-schoolers. Also, such programs can grow with the child.

- **Are there help screens or prompts?** These are aids for confused users. Sometimes, typing the word "help," the letter "H," or even a "?" will take you to one of these help screens. Children don't want to wait for you to look up directions in the manual every time you begin a new program.

- **How readable or necessary is the program's manual?** It should be brief, with fairly large type. It should have ideas and suggestions for supplementary activities away from the computer. And even if these ideas don't appeal to you, they often lead to other ideas.

  Necessary program explanations are often accomplished best by including *screen shots* (photos of what the actual screen looks like). Ideally, the manual should be almost unnecessary for pre-school programs. Instead, the user should be led through on-screen documentation; i.e., help screens, prompts, simple menus, and icons.

  Some manuals come with extras like coloring books and stickers. Kids love 'em. The STICKYBEAR series from WEEKLY READER FAMILY SOFTWARE comes with a hardcover book, stickers, and a poster. And Raquel says proudly, "I know my shapes. I do shapes in my shape book."

- **What responses does the program give for incorrect answers?** Hit some incorrect keys and watch what happens. Is it more fun to be wrong than right? Are there more bells and whistles for incorrect responses? Does a wrong answer produce an obnoxious razzing sound or some other inappropriate response that tells everybody within earshot that the child blew it? What kind of response does the program make for continued incorrect answers to the same questions?

EARLY GAMES (SPRINGBOARD) has a program called COUNT that displays, for example, three small squares, one after another, with an accompanying beep, beep, beep. The child is to type the numeral three. A wrong answer causes the squares to beep again, this time changing color as they do so. A second wrong answer causes the beeping numerals 1, 2, and 3 to appear and disappear one at a time inside each of the boxes. Another incorrect response causes the musical numerals to appear again, this time remaining in view. Yet another error makes the numerals 1, 2, and 3 flash several times in their respective boxes as they beep. One more strike and you're out. The program, after giving the child five tries, finally displays a very large numeral three, then goes on to another, simpler problem.

- **Is the program forgiving?** That is, can you recover from errors without "crashing" your program? Children are likely to hit inappropriate keys accidentally while trying to strike other keys. (Diana accidentally hits the space bar about three out of every five attempts.) Hit some totally inappropriate keys. Is the consequence likely to be a problem for you?

SOME OTHER CONSIDERATIONS

I like programs that encourage vocabulary development. As a teacher with sixteen years of stamina to my credit, I am continually distressed by students who ask to borrow the "foot stick" or ask permission to go to the library to get an "H." With parent and child working through a good pre-school program several times, "you mail it" becomes "letter," "Yikes!" becomes "dragon," and "jammies" becomes "pajamas." (And the *child's* vocabulary usually improves, too!)

I think kids are great fun to be with. Working at the computer is merely an excuse for me to spend time with the children. Thus, I enjoy programs that can be used as "conversation pieces." Indeed, children's comments are often . . .

Perceptive: "We're real and Miss Piggy's pretend, right Paggy?"

Informative: "I ride a tamel once at the Bronts Zoo— and I sat right on the lump!"

Relative: "That's a ostrich—he's Big Bird's cousin."

Energetic: "I just gotta wake my muscles up. I want to wake 'em up so I can hold heavy stuff."

To the point: "I'm tired. I think I'll take a two-minute break-down."

Sexy: "Is this a girl computer or a boy computer?" (Devony once pointed out that, "It *must* be a boy computer, cause it does mistakes!")

I like programs that "computer-safe" children can use alone, as well as together with parents. Although I prefer programs that lend themselves to cooperative play, I believe that children sometimes need to work independently. And sometimes parents simply don't have the time to work with them.

I like programs that are *different* from what goes on in school—programs that use the computer as a playful medium. (Children often say "Let's play computer.") In a very heavy discussion a few years ago, my son Joseph, then six years old, put his finger right on the problem. "School is boring," he declared. "Especially when you have to color an elephant." Very profound—and this from the same kid who wanted to know if we get water from water buffaloes.

I like "adult" programs that can be used with kids, especially those that produce printouts that can be shared with friends and relatives. No matter what Raquel does on the computer, she always comments, "Maybe Grammy will like it." Simple word processors and programs like the previously-mentioned PRINT SHOP and MASK PARADE are favorites of mine. I also enjoy a lot of the art and music software (see Chapter 7).

Very young children can do some interesting and creative things with computers (especially when the adults in their lives heap generous amounts of praise upon them). That's because they're pretty interesting and creative little people. Use the tips in this chapter to pick out some exciting software to use with your children. You'll probably help each other to learn a great deal. Moreover, an added bonus is that your time spent together will be very satisfying. In the final analysis, the effectiveness of the software or of any teaching tool depends on the people using it. Thus, when Joseph came home from school one day with a report announcing that "his spelling is improved and his writing is neat and *ledigle*," I knew that we were in for a tough year.

The computer is just one more interesting aspect of the adult world for kids to figure out. After several of our computer sessions, Devony began to "practice" at home. She would type on her toy touch-tone telephone and scribble with pencil on paper.

"What are you doing, Devony?" her grandmother asked one day.

"Oh, I'm working on my computer and taking notes like Paggy. Only one problem, though," she added, "I don't have any discos."

I am amazed at how much very young children understand and how much they are capable of understanding, as long as we help them to make sense of their world.

Organizations that Evaluate Software

Educational Products Information Exchange (EPIE), P.O. Box 839, Water Mill, NY 11976. Also features EPIE ON-LINE, an electronically-accessible software evaluating service (you need a modem to contact them via telephone and computer).

International Council for Computers in Education, Department of Computer and Information Science, University of Oregon, 1787 Agate Street, Eugene, OR 97403. David Moursand, author of *Parent's Guide to Computers in Education,* heads this organization of computer educators.

Minnesota Educational Computing Corp. (MECC), 3490 Lexington Ave., St. Paul, MN 55112. Features newsletters, a help line, and publications such as *Educational Computing Catalogue.*

For your consideration, we present three pieces of evidence as to how smart kids really are.

Exhibit A

An extremely verbal pre-schooler informed a grown-up friend that, "The Santa Claus at Child World isn't real."

"He's not?" questioned the adult.

"Oh, no!" replied the child, "He's just a man dressed up in a Santa Claus suit."

"Why, I had no idea!" exclaimed the grown-up.

"Oh, sure! You didn't know that? *Everybody* knows that. The real one's at Bradlees."

Exhibit B

A kindergartener wanted to know why her friend's cat had kittens while her own had none. "Why, your cat has no Daddy, silly," said her friend. Not wanting to appear stupid, she decided to wait until she got home to ask Mom and Dad about this.

That evening, at dinner, she asked, "What does having a Daddy cat have to do with having kittens?" Before Mom or Dad could answer, her seven-year-old brother chimed in with, "Sis, they'll tell you when you're older—but you'll *never* believe it!"

Exhibit C

One first-grader heard the word "prostitute" in school and asked her mother what it meant. Struggling for an answer, Mom finally replied, "A prostitute is . . . a woman who . . . goes out with men for money."

"Oh," replied the little girl, "You mean like a hooker?"

4

Keyboard Alternatives

This chapter is a survey of devices allowing kids and computers to "communicate" without a keyboard. Many pre-schoolers simply don't have the manual dexterity or mental acuity to operate the conventional keyboard, with its maze of numbers, letters, punctuation marks, symbols, and control keys. Keyboard alternatives, then, are computer input devices that allow kids to circumvent the keyboard. With these devices, it is the software, once again, that is crucial. So, carefully examine both the keyboard alternative and the software that drives it before handing over your money.

MUPPET LEARNING KEYS

Muppet Learning Keys, by SUNBURST COMMUNICATIONS, is a keyboard designed especially for kids (the packaging declares, "For Kids Three and Up"). It features large, alphabetically-arranged keys, a paint box with eight colors, a ruler—the familiar contents of a school desk. The keys are soft plastic, slightly raised "membrane" keys—the kind featured on many microwave ovens. Ingeniously designed, Muppet Keys is lightweight, weighing about three pounds, but quite durable. It is plugged into your computer's game port via a seven-foot cord, allowing for set-up on the floor or on a child's lap.

Muppet Learning Keys comes with a disk entitled, THE MUPPET DISCOVERY DISK. This is a number and letter recognition program that's a lot of fun. It includes several activities—

DISCOVERY STAGE, LETTERS STAGE, and NUMBERS STAGE. All are entertaining, but the best part is that our Muppet friends are cleverly woven into the product. For example, Miss Piggy is displayed on the "Help" key tied to the railroad tracks, making it the "HELP!" key.

The children I worked with liked DISCOVERY STAGE best. Striking any alphabet key produces a picture of something whose name begins with that letter. The letter B causes a Bird to appear. Tap a number 6 on the ruler and six birds appear. Touch the blue membrane key in the paint box and the six birds turn blue. Gazing at the six blue birds on our screen, I asked Diana, "Do you have any birdies around your house?" "No," she answered. "I have a hippo-pot-a-mus."

Tap the GO key and the objects become musically-animated. The letter E produces an Elephant, and GO causes it to squirt water over its body.

"He's taking a shower!" shouted Diana.

"Do you take showers?" I asked her.

"No."

"How do you get clean, then?"

"By a towel."

Bret pressed S and 3 and GO and viewed 3 musical Socks. "Do your socks sing?" I asked, trying to be funny. "No," said Bret seriously. "Does yours?" Later, I asked Matthew if *his* socks sang. Without batting an eyelash, he declared, "Yep!"

Some of the color schemes that can be produced with THE MUPPET DISCOVERY DISK are unusual. "Who ever saw purple walruses?" I asked Raquel. "I did," she told me, "at Child World."

Max pressed the letter F and a small Fireplace with burning wood appeared. Since green was the last color selected, we had a green fire. "Look Max," I said, ". . . green fire." "Yeh," said Max matter-of-factly. "they must be burning green wood."

The letter G produces a Ghost, and Raquel tells me—"It's in my room, sometimes—not all the time—I hiding!" Diana, harboring similar feelings ("I don't like ghosts!") discovered a practical solution. She pressed the conveniently-placed Muppet ERASE key (in the form of a rubber eraser, of course), completely clearing the screen. She then informed me that, "I didn't see *Ghost Busters*. My sister did. I stayed at Nonie's."

Muppet Learning Keys

Another handy key is the STOP key, which displays Fozzie Bear holding a stop sign. If you want to discontinue the animation/sound, you should press Fozzie's stop sign. When Max became tired of his green fire, he tapped the STOP key. But for some reason he was unable to activate the switch. There was either a temporary malfunction or else he wasn't pressing the key properly. In any case, he frantically pressed keys trying to get the blaze under control. When he finally did, he proclaimed, "I'm Smokey the Bear!"

The LETTERS STAGE calls for the user to identify letters. A letter appears on the screen and the child must locate and press the corresponding key. Once, an X appeared on the screen and I directed Max to "Find the X." He immediately pointed to the X on our screen and said, "Right there!"

Although the letters appear in alphabetical order from left to right, and the children are able to recite the alphabet, locating letters takes some getting used to. It seems that this left-to-right arrangement isn't inherently logical—it's just an arbitrary convention that our society has adopted. Once children get accustomed to that left-to-rightness, though, they accept it as quite natural. Recently, when Emma, a six-year-old with three years of computing experience, was struggling with the conventional keyboard, she asked her dad, "Why don't they put these keys in order?"

The NUMBERS STAGE teaches beginning counting skills. Objects appear on the screen and the child must add them up and press the appropriate number key. Most of my pre-school friends can count, but they have little sense of what those numbers actually mean. Hence, Bethy once told her mother, "I love you five times as much and Dad two times as much—which is more?" When Mother informed her daughter that five times was greater, she reconsidered. "Oh," said Bethy. "Then I love Dad five times as much and you two times as much . . . but you both do a commendable job."

Bethy has a clear focus on the world, even if her grasp of numbers isn't fully developed yet. Thus, when five queens showed up on our screen and I asked her who the boss would be if there were five queens, she replied, "the king, of course."

Muppet Keys and, particularly, the DISCOVERY STAGE of the MUPPET DISCOVERY DISK, have considerable "staying power"—children don't get tired of them quickly. A number of "Parent Control Options" serve to increase that staying power. These allow parents to set the Letters and Numbers Stages to just upper- or just lower-case letters, and to make the letters/numbers appear in sequence or at random.

If Cammie's kids are using another program and happen to see the keyboard on a shelf, they often call out, "Can I do Muppet Keys, please?" Once they get started on Muppet Keys, they don't want to quit. "Can I show you something?" I asked Emily, intently changing red dancing alligators into blue singing pretzels. "No," she answered curtly. And when I asked Diana if she wanted to give her sister, Danielle, a turn, she reluctantly said, "Otay." But then she turned to her sister and cautioned, "You can't use it *all*!" It's probably Bethy who best sums up the kids' feelings when she asks, "Can I share alone?"

The Muppet Keys package sells for $79.95. SUNBURST manufactures additional software (TEDDY'S PLAYGROUND and GETTING READY TO READ AND ADD) that makes use of The Muppet Keys. Independent software manufacturers are working on programs that will also make use of the keyboard. CBS's ASTRO-GROVER and DR. SEUSS FIX-UP THE MIX-UP PUZZLER, and THE LEARNING COMPANY's READER RABBIT, are the first of these.

A clever promotional ad claims that "Muppet Keys is to the standard computer keyboard what the tricycle is to the bicycle." This may be true. All I can say is that pre-schoolers really take to these "training wheels!"

Currently, SUNBURST COMMUNICATIONS (39 Washington Ave., Pleasantville, NY 10570, 800-431-1934) makes models that run on Apple IIe, IIc, Commodore 64, Commodore 128, and IBM PCjr. In addition, SUNBURST provides an Apple II and Apple II + Adaptor ($9.95), which allows those machines to interface with the Muppet Learning Keys. A disk drive is required and a color monitor is "highly recommended." Some Muppet Keys drawbacks: the colors red and yellow are not very vivid when produced via Apple computers. Also, some favorite Muppets (like Bert, Ernie, and Big Bird) are conspicuously absent.

JOYSTICKS

A joystick is a popular hand-held input device first used for "shoot-em-up" computer games. It has two main parts—a handle and a button or two (or three). The handle is used to move your gun/cannon/laser beam into position and the button(s) for firing. But newer programs make use of the joystick in less violent ways. The handle (usually in the center of the device) can control the position of the cursor, allowing you to point at and select icons or menu items. Joysticks are also used in many art/drawing/graphics programs. MASK PARADE and THE PRINT SHOP can utilize joysticks as input devices. Indeed, some programs, when loaded into the computer's memory, first ask which input device you will be using—keyboard, joystick, touch tablet, etc.

Programs are increasingly making liberal use of icons. Joysticks and icons go pretty well together. Some programs line up icons along the left side of the screen, allowing for a natural up and down movement of the joystick handle to select them.

Joystick

Logically, you point to the DISK icon when you want to save what you are working on. You point to the TRASH BARREL icon when you want to clear your work space and start something new. You point to the PRINTER icon to print out your master-piece.

Pre-schoolers need time to get accustomed to joystick opera-tion, and some never quite get the hang of it. Many have trouble manipulating the handle, and most find it awkward to hold onto the device with one hand and press a button with the other. The pre-schoolers I worked with experienced only limited success, but elementary school kids have little trouble with them. My little charges would contort their bodies and grimace as they tried to accurately direct the cursor. At times I thought they would break the handle right off the device—as if they had just made a wish over Thanksgiving dinner and were determined to snap that bone.

There are numerous brands of joysticks. If you decide to buy one, be sure to select one that runs on your machine. The price is usually anywhere from $10.00 to $50.00. There are many independent manufacturers. In addition, computer companies such as Apple, Atari, Commodore, IBM, and Tandy/Radio Shack manufacture joysticks.

TOUCH TABLETS

Touch tablets are graphics devices. The one we use at Cammie's Day Care Home is the KoalaPad touch tablet (KOALA TECHNOLOGIES, 2065 Junction Ave., San Jose, CA 95131, 408-946-4483; 800-562-2327). It is plugged right into your computer via a four-foot cord, allowing for placement of the tablet on the user's lap. It comes with an excellent software package, called KoalaPainter. Adults and older children can create charts, graphs, and cartoons (a color monitor is necessary to appreciate

Touch tablet

its capabilities) that can be printed out. Pre-schoolers can draw, doodle, and point (to make selections from screen choices).

The KoalaPad is a 6″ × 8″ plastic base with about a 4″ square pressure-sensitive area. Making sketches on the "touch-sensitive" surface with a stylus (provided) or finger (you must supply your own) produces those sketches on the screen. Also, touching the stylus or finger to the tablet moves the cursor to select menu choices or icons. There are two large buttons at the top of the pad for selecting options.

A touch tablet allows you to draw freehand with different "brushes." The stylus is about the size of a regular pen. (Perhaps a "fatter" one would be more manageable for tots.) Most kids I worked with like the stylus, but Bethy usually started out drawing with it, then put it over her ear and sketched with her finger. You can control the width, shape, and color of the lines to be drawn. This drawing is a natural motion, and going back and forth between menu options and drawing area became second nature to our four-year-olds. I observed a definite state of "diminishing returns," however, as the age of the artists got younger. This was true of our entire computing experience, though I'm sure all the children I worked with enjoyed and benefited from using computers.

Other software that makes use of the touch tablet as an input device is available. KoalaPad offers PAINT-A-RHYME and KOALAGRAMS (both for Apple and Commodore) for the "early learner" set. PAINT-A-RHYME is a computer coloring book with music. Children can "paint" any of thirty nursery rhyme pictures. KOALAGRAMS is a beginning spelling program that requires no keyboard input.

The KoalaPad touch tablet comes with clear, brief instructions that no one ever reads. It's just so much fun to figure out yourself—and it lends itself so nicely to the trial-and-error approach. It runs on the Apple II series, Atari Home Computers, Commodore 64, and IBM PC/PCjr. The cost is $125 for the Apple and PCjr, $150 for the IBM PC, $99 for the Atari and Commodore.

SUNCOM, INC. (260 Holbrook Drive, Wheeling, IL 60090) manufactures touch tablets for the Commodore ($89.95) and the Apple ($99.95). In addition, SUNCOM is working on versions for Atari and IBM.

MOUSE POINTING DEVICES

A "computer" mouse is an input device the size of a cigarette pack that also connects to your computer by a cable and interface card. It rolls on a kind of ball-bearing. The idea is to clear a small space next to your computer over which you can move the mouse. Moving the mouse across your desktop (that is, rolling it via the ball-bearing) controls the position of the cursor. As my fellow computer club members tell me, your hand/mouse movements become "translated by an internal optical sensor into cursor movements." As with the touch tablet, there is a button (or two, or three) for selecting icons/menu choices. Pushing the mouse button is referred to as "clicking."

You can also sketch with the mouse (Apple's mouse comes with software called MOUSEPAINT). This is accomplished by holding the mouse button down while dragging the mouse across the workspace. This is not as natural as sketching with a stylus, but children get used to it in a short time. Again, the "older" children (four and up) get the hang of it more quickly. The younger ones tend to call it Mickey Mouse and want to give it a piece of cheese. Four-year-old Bret likes to doodle with his mouse on the family's Apple IIC computer. He and his mom use MOUSEPAINT and a similar program from BRODER-BUND (see Chapter 7 for the address) called DAZZLEDRAW. Bret especially enjoys using the mouse to select different shapes and then fill them with bright colors.

The Apple Mouse II with MOUSEPAINT makes great use of color. It sells for $149. IBM also features several versions of mice with software similar to MOUSEPAINT. Prices range from $175 to $220.

Mouse

LIGHT PENS

A light pen is yet another "draw & point" device that helps the user to get around the intimidation of the keyboard. Computer-savvy parents who write simple education programs claim that it is ideal for their pre-schoolers—all the children have to do is point to the correct answer.

Overall, the light pen is very natural as an art tool or menu-selector. Like other keyboard alternatives, it is plugged into the computer and connected by a thin cable. It allows you to draw and "paint" right on the computer screen. The screen has always been a good "canvas." Now, light pens and touch tablets have emerged as good "paintbrushes."

The Gibson Light Pen from KOALA TECHNOLOGIES (KOALA, as you can see, is big on keyboard alternatives) resembles a regular pen in size and shape. As with the touch tablet stylus, pre-schoolers might better enjoy an oversized one with flat edges (like the crayons we used to have in kindergarten— you know, the ones that wouldn't roll off the desk). Another problem with light pens is that kids get tired of holding them up to the screen. My friend, an avid computer hobbyist with three computer-using daughters (triplets who began computing at the age of three) came up with a neat solution. He tipped the screen over on its "back" to make the drawing surface more natural for his daughters.

An annoying problem for some pre-school artists is the sensitivity of the pen. Lines are sometimes drawn not quite when and where the artist wants them. This can be a source of frustration for pre-schoolers, but in general light pens are great fun—and powerful ones, like those from KOALA TECHNOLOGIES, can be "grown into" over a period of time.

The accompanying documentation is well-written. Our Gibson Light Pen arrived via UPS one Friday. My twelve-year-old son, James, figured it out by trial-and-error. He spent several hours fiddling with it on Friday evening and another few hours over the weekend. He used the manual only sparingly. Later, he explained the whole operation to me in about twenty minutes. Thank goodness for computer-savvy kids—how else would parent/computer writers survive? This is especially true when you consider the fact that, if it took James eight hours to become

Light pen

familiar with the device, it would have taken me about sixteen (a conservative estimate).

The Gibson Light Pen ($249.95) runs on Apple II, II Plus, and IIe computers. It comes with two disks, PENPAINTER and PENDESIGNER. These are pretty sophisticated packages suitable for architectural design as well as doodling. Pre-schoolers will need to have a parent handy (for coaching and to help read some on-screen directions). PENMUSICIAN (on the PENPAINTER disk) even helps you to compose or learn to read music. You point the pen at musical notes and select them by pressing the space bar. You then point the pen to one of three on-screen musical staff lines to place them into position. When done, you point to the Play option. The correct rhythm and pitch for each note comes singing out of your computer. When James has trouble reading a piece of his piano music he sets it up on PENMUSICIAN, then plays it back to himself. He can then hear the correct rhythm via the computer keyboard and return to the piano keyboard.

KOALA TECHNOLOGIES also produces the Koala Light
Pen for use on the Commodore and Atari computers. The price
is $99. TECH-SKETCH INC. (26 Just Road, Fairfield, NJ
07006) manufactures light pens for use with Apple, Atari, and
Commodore computers. These range in price from $34.95 to
$49.95.

"Cheese, mouse."

5

Kid-Proofing Your Computer Station

The best precautions you can take for your equipment are: (1) keeping an organized computer work station, and (2) keeping your child company at the keyboard. "A place for everything and everything in its place," and "no toddlers may solo here" are two mottos to live by. If those sentiments are taken to heart, and you secure an insurance policy that covers computer hardware and software (see end of this chapter for list of companies), you should be able to sleep nights.

NO EATING, DRINKING, OR SMOKING ALLOWED

This includes toddlers munching on such appetizing peripherals as joysticks. Make sure *everyone* obeys this rule and children will learn right from the start that this is what is expected in the computer room. Food and drink near disks, computer hardware, and pre-schoolers are open invitations to disaster. Post-schoolers have been known to spill a cocktail or two on various peripherals, as well. Disks also seem to be particularly susceptible to damage from cigarette smoke.

OUT OF SIGHT—OUT OF MIND

Keep things that you don't want touched out of sight, in file drawers or other compartments. If you don't want your child to touch the disks, take them out of their attractive Muppets packages. Then he can fondle Big Bird's likeness to his heart's content. Put the disks in a key-lock container, lock it, and let the child fondle that for a while, too, until he loses interest in it.

THOU SHALT BACK UP THY SOFTWARE

Make back-up copies (duplicates) of all software. Some software programs come with a back-up. Others come with an on-disk copy program that allows you to make one copy of the program. Unfortunately, none of the approximately forty pre-school software programs that I reviewed includes either of these features. Therefore, making back-ups may require purchasing copy programs like LOCKSMITH, NIBBLES AWAY, or COPY II PLUS. Copyright law allows *only* the purchaser of a software program to make *only* one copy, and *only* for his personal use. This copy is called an *archival copy*. Keep back-ups separate from the originals so that one disaster won't ruin both. Also, it is a good idea to use the back-ups on a regular basis, storing the originals in a safe place.

COMPLETE THY PAPERWORK

Most reputable manufacturers will supply free replacement copies of defective or "bombed" disks within, say, ninety days, and will replace "user-damaged" disks for a minimal fee after ninety days. (See the warranty policies of programs in Chapter 7.)

You should always fill out and return all warranty cards (for hardware *and* software). Some computer companies offer a service plan beyond the warranty period. So check it out.

EASY DOES IT—
THEY'RE FLOPPY, BUT DON'T BEND 'EM!

Teach the children to handle disks and computer equipment carefully. Do not touch the magnetic surface of a disk. Do not fold, bend, or otherwise mutilate disks. As might be expected, toddlers are innately adept at disk mutilation. Keep disks away from dust, smoke, food, drink, extremes of temperature, and sources of magnetism. Store disks upright in their disk jackets, but don't pack them together too tightly. You can keep them free of dust and grime by storing them in boxes. (You should consider dust covers for your hardware, too.) If you must write on a disk label, use a felt-tipped marker—never a ballpoint pen or pencil. The pressure of a pen point can affect the disk's magnetic data.

When you think they are ready, walk the children through the various steps of careful computer use: handling a disk by its label, inserting it carefully into the drive, closing the door gingerly, and turning the computer on gently. With the youngest children, it may be best to master each of these tasks one at a time. When the child shows you that he can handle a disk carefully, teach him how to insert it into the drive. Once he has the motor control to insert a disk properly, show him how to close the disk drive door. Next, teach him how to turn the machine on and off.

It is a good idea to teach children not to insert or remove disks from disk drives while the drives are spinning. Although some manuals state that this practice is acceptable, the chances are good that a child will destroy the disk in the process.

It's also a good idea to get every family computer user into the habit of: (1) returning disks to their protective jackets, and (2) returning them to their proper places. If you put the disks back into their original packaging, even non-reading children will learn to recognize "their" disks. Another alternative is to put the children's disks in separate, large envelopes with appropriate, easily-recognizable pictures or symbols pasted on the outside.

NO TOYS OR PETS ALLOWED

Keep toys out of the computer room. Who knows what dangers lurk therein (magnets, or metal objects that may have become magnetized)? Pets, too, are a computer room no-no. Computer equipment is too fragile, too costly to chance accidents because of a frisky animal. The computer, Mom and Dad, brothers, sisters, and friends, are enough playmates for this room.

NO DROOLING ALLOWED

Slobbering and/or drooling on electrical objects should be dealt with impulsively. One parent told me about his highly-innovative and successful kid-proofing secret—he wrapped the entire keyboard in a clear plastic bag. This is an ideal interface between drooling toddlers with messy hands and the keyboard. For best results, the bag should be changed after every three thousand miles or one puncture—whichever comes first.

POSITION EQUIPMENT WITH THE TODDLER IN MIND

A curious child, while trying to tear off a piece of computer paper, can accidentally send an ill-placed printer tumbling to the floor. So be sure to align computer components with your child's eye level in mind.

Try to tape or tie up exposed power cords so that they are out of sight as much as possible. This will keep children from tripping over them. It will also make them less inviting to a toddler's touch.

Try to get at your toddler's eye level to determine what "out of sight" is. A friend of mine, who has a Franklin Ace Computer and a two and a half-year-old daughter who loves computers, has a small problem. The first thing she sees as she approaches the Ace is the RESET button, which is on the bottom left of the keyboard. Because it's a flashy orange button, it catches her eye just as she nears the machine, yelling, "Play 'puter Dad—play 'puter!" Then she ends up resetting the thing every six seconds!

NO ROUGHHOUSING ALLOWED

Using terms like "easy does it" and "gently now" will get toddlers accustomed to the kind of behavior that is expected in this room. Other rooms, as well as the outdoors, are designed for more active play.

To acquaint children with gently striking one key at a time, you might give them access to an old typewriter (electric, if possible—you can find inexpensive, working relics at yard sales and flea markets), or an old touch telephone. For reasons of safety, you may want to remove the phone's cord. In any case, it should be disconnected before a child plays with it. My sister Claire, a telephone operator for twenty-five years, reminds me of the many emergency calls that operators handle, and cautions that, "An operating telephone is *not* a toy!"

WHAT TO CONSIDER WHEN PURCHASING A COMPUTER DESK OR TABLE

Look for sturdiness. Give the furniture a few good shoves from several different angles. It shouldn't shake or vibrate in the least. Don't try to pinch pennies on a table or desk. It doesn't make sense to spend $1000 or more on computer hardware and $12.95 on a flimsy desk to support it. Accidents are even more likely with youngsters around, so we need to take every possible precaution. You may want to consider converting an old table or desk into a computer station. Remember to consider stability first—Aunt Martha's bridge table might be great for card games, but collapsible table legs, computers, and kids make for a dangerous combination.

Look for enough desktop space to accommodate all your hardware (computer, monitor, disk drive), with space left over to write on or to move a mouse around. The more desktop space, the better. You may buy additional hardware later (like a printer) and may need more desktop space. Plan ahead.

Look for leg room. Consider the fact that a child might be sitting on your lap or that several people might sit side by side at the keyboard. A large table often provides more leg room than a desk. The trade-off is that, with a table, you'll sacrifice drawer space.

Consider also that standard table or desktop height may be uncomfortable for a child working at the keyboard. Some computers have detachable keyboards connected to the computer by a cable. These keyboards solve the height problem because they can be placed on the child's lap. Otherwise, you might opt for shaving the table's legs or for adjustable chairs, or even for computer stands or desks with adjustable height features.

SETTING UP

Be sure to place the table or desk against a wall to minimize the chances of a child knocking peripherals to the floor. Make sure, however, that the computer has "breathing room." Some computers have vents that help dissipate heat build-up. These vents need open air space for proper ventilation.

Choose a place in the room that is away from heaters, not too close to a television (the computer can cause TV interference), and away from rugs (possible static problems). Static seems to build up during winter in hot, dry rooms. You can combat this by treating your rug with an anti-static spray or by installing a humidifier or a static mat.

Position lighting so as to minimize glare off the screen. Keep at least eighteen inches between the screen and the child. This is enough distance to keep radiation exposure at low levels, but still allows a child to point to objects on the screen.

Purchase a power strip (a device that accepts six to eight plugs) with a built-in "surge suppressor." This accommodates all the cords you will need to plug in and protects against electrical power surges or "spikes" that may damage your hardware. Don't plug other appliances into the same outlet as your computer or power strip. For safety ideas, browse through a computer equipment manufacturer's catalog. (Schools are inundated with these catalogs—do your local high school a favor and take one off their hands.) They feature office furniture as well as items such as WIRE AWAY, CORD COVER, ANTI-STATIC FLOOR MATS, and SCREENWIPE.

Plan your work station thoughtfully. If it is to double as an adult work station (with correspondingly longer keyboard sessions), be advised that many complaints about backaches and eyestrain after work at the CRT are due to a poorly-designed work station.

Devise a lay-out that will accommodate all your software, books, manuals, and keyboard alternatives. As in the rest of the house, the computer room tends to collect volumes of "important stuff."

Allow for some flexibility in positioning equipment. You may find, after experimenting for a while, that some rearranging of peripherals is necessary. Don't lock yourself into any one set-up.

I used all of the preceding ideas in building my own computer station. I have included the instructions for building it (written for the novice tool-user, like myself) in the Appendix. Give it a look—it's really quite simple, and superior to any table or desk arrangement that I have yet seen. If the project seems too ambitious a task, purchase a computer desk or table and use my computer stations as a model. "Steal" whatever ideas you like.

INSURE YOUR HARDWARE AND SOFTWARE

The following insurance companies offer special policies that cover both computer hardware and software. You may want to compare what they offer with what provisions you may be able to add on to your homeowner's policy.

Continental Insurance, 2 Corporate Place S., Piscataway, NJ 08854; 201-981-4224.

Fireman's Fund, 777 San Marin Drive, Novato, CA 94998; 415-899-2647.

Nationwide, 1 Nationwide Plaza, Columbus, OH 43216; 614-227-7111.

Safeware, The Insurance Agency, Inc., 2929 N. High St., Columbus, OH 43202; 614-262-0559.

"Wheeee!"

6

Computer-Proofing Your Kid

The best safety precaution you can take is to make sure young children are never in the computer room unsupervised. Making the computing experience a *family* experience ensures safety as well as family fun. As an added precaution, you might wish to place a collapsible safety gate at the computer room's entrance, to keep "unauthorized toddlers" out.

THE COMPUTER IS AN ELECTRICAL APPLIANCE

Remember that the computer is an electrical appliance and should be treated as such. Keep liquids away—that means no food or drinks in the computer room. Keep wires out of sight, out of mind (and also out of mouth—chewing on electrical wires is a definite no-no!). The easiest way to keep wires out of sight is to wind them into a small bundle and then attach them to the back of the counter or to the wall with tape. Eliminating excess wire will also help prevent a child from tripping. Some office supply companies sell wire storage devices that help control the power cord tangle. When determining what is out of sight, get down to your child's level—eye level, that is. While you're at it, take a crawling tour of the room, placing "taboo" objects out of view. In this way, you won't have to stifle the child's curiosity by repeatedly saying "NO!"

You should also avoid opening the lid of your computer when toddlers are around. Don't give them any ideas about poking around inside computers. If you do need to tinker with your computer (say, to adjust an interface card), take the following steps:

1. Banish all toddlers from the room.

2. Shut off the power switch but leave the computer plugged in (this ensures proper grounding).

3. Remove the computer's lid.

4. Before touching any inner components, ground yourself by first touching the computer's power supply. This will discharge any static electricity that you may have acquired. This important precaution can prevent your computer chips from shorting out. More importantly, Step 1 above will keep your toddler from shorting out. Actually, computer club members tell me that the voltage in today's computers is low, with relatively little danger to humans. One exception is the CRT (monitor), which requires high voltage.

NO TOYS IN THE COMPUTER ROOM

Obviously, some of the same techniques that help protect your hardware also help protect your child.

The "No Toys" rule will ensure that the child has no distractions and nothing in his hands to toss at the screen, or through it! It will also reinforce the notion that this room is not a playroom. Instead, roughhousing and active play are discouraged, and learning and quiet play are the order of the day.

SECURING COMPUTER COMPONENTS

Inquisitive toddlers can easily pull computers, monitors, or other objects down upon themselves. Children trying to tear their printouts from the rest of the computer paper could conceivably bring the printer tumbling down as well. In addition, because of rapidly-moving parts, the print heads on some printers heat up to temperatures sufficient to burn a child's skin. So position computer components with these things in mind. Try to make the keyboard very accessible, the drives less so, and the printer even less so. Place the monitor in a spot where light from windows does not fall directly on it and reflections from lights won't shine in the child's eyes.

CHILD-PROOFING TECHNIQUES IN THE COMPUTER ROOM

It is better to have rounded rather than sharp edges on all furniture. Note the molded edge on our counter top in the Appendix. At least bumps are better than cuts in the event that an unstable toddler falls. You should also place plastic safety caps on unused electric sockets, to discourage tiny exploring fingers. Finally, use safety latches on cupboards and file drawers that you want to keep free from little inquisitive hands. KINDERGARD and SAFE-T-LATCH are two popular manufacturers of such items. They help keep potentially harmful items and children away from each other.

Rethink your safety precautions as your child progresses from one developmental stage to the next (i.e., crawling, walking, climbing, etc.). The trick is to always try to stay one stage ahead of your child.

BRIEF KEYBOARD SESSIONS

Many computer-related health complaints in the adult workplace may be attributed to too much time at the keyboard. The National Institute of Occupational Safety and Health (NISH), which investigates such things as eye fatigue, cataracts, and the effects of VDT (Video Display Terminal) use on pregnant women, recommends a 15-minute break after each hour at the computer.

RADIATION

Color televisions and monitors produce radiation in the form of light, ultraviolet light, and X-rays. Even four-year-old Raquel knows "X-ray is dandrus—you can't touch it."

The risk of exposing their children to radiation is a big concern for many computer-age parents. However, experts disagree as to just how much radiation is emitted by TVs and monitors and how harmful exposure is.

The amount of radiation given off by TVs, monitors, microwave ovens, and other appliances is negligible, according to most of the vested interests. "You get more radiation in one dentist's X-ray than you do in months of TV-watching," says a local television salesman. My dentist says, "You get more radiation from the sun each day than you do in a decade of X-rays." Maybe so—still, I'd avoid long, frequent sessions at the keyboard. Go outside for some fresh air. Play ball, read a book, go to the beach. A healthy attitude is fostered when children become competent at and enjoy using computers, realizing also that there are many other things in the world worth doing, too.

We know that color monitors emit more radiation than monochrome sets (color requires higher voltages). We also know that radiation follows the *Inverse Square Law*. Basically, this means that the farther away you are from the source of radiation, the safer you are. In more sophisticated jargon, the radiation decreases as the square of the distance. This inverse square stuff is one of my favorites, since it's one of the few complicated-sounding pieces of science that I'm able to understand.

If you are, for example, twelve inches from the screen, you receive a certain dose of radiation. If you double that distance (twenty-four inches from the screen), the dose of radiation is now one-fourth of what it was. (You multiplied the distance by two—the square of two is four, therefore radiation becomes one-fourth.) If you triple the distance (thirty-six inches) the radiation becomes one-ninth. (You multiplied the distance by three—the square of three is nine, therefore radiation becomes one-ninth.) You may want to position the chair or bench as far from the screen as is practical. Computers with detachable keyboards, such as the IBM PCjr, are ideal for this. (NOTE: The computer station in the Appendix provides about twenty inches between user and monitor, and can be adjusted to allow for even more distance.)

Radiation exposure is cumulative. Therefore, in addition to the distance from the source of radiation, the *length of time* that you are exposed determines the amount of radiation you receive. Of course, for any given distance, the longer you are exposed to a source of radiation, the greater the total radiation.

Manufacturers of early TVs and the first CRTs paid less attention to radiation emission. More recently, manufacturers have altered design to ensure lower emission levels. (Solid state technology represents a major safety improvement.) So the wisest thing to do is to opt for newer equipment, while avoiding both sitting too close to the screen and prolonged sessions at the keyboard.

Finally, you may want to consider purchasing a radiation screen (lead-impregnated acrylic safety shield—see below for manufacturer addresses). These shields are designed to be placed in front of the CRT, blocking harmful radiation.

COMPANIES THAT MANUFACTURE SAFETY DEVICES

Biflyx/Design West, 2532 Dupont Dr., Irvine, CA 92715

I-Protect, 301 N. Prairie Ave., Suite 510, Inglewood, CA 90301

Langley-St. Clair Instrumentation Systems, 132 W. 24th St., New York, NY 10011

Technograph, 356 McRae Dr., Toronto, Ontario, M46 1T5, Canada

"What do you want to play with today, Muffy? Astro-grover, Dr. Seuss or Charlie Brown's A-B-Cs?"

7

A Toddler's Software Sampler

There is an incredible array of "small fry" software programs on the market today. This chapter will briefly review those that I am familiar with. The following programs are listed alphabetically under their manufacturers. In the event that a program you are interested in is not readily available, you might contact the manufacturer to find out where it can be purchased. Please note also that prices mentioned here (as well as throughout the book) are subject to change.

Manufacturer: ADVANCED IDEAS, INC.
Address: 2902 San Pablo Ave., Berkeley, CA 94702
Telephone: 415-526-9100
Warranty Policy: Free replacement within 12 months of purchase. A $10.00 charge thereafter.

Program Name: DINOSAURS
Hardware: Versions for Apple, Commodore.
Suggested Ages: 2½ to 5
Documentation: 24-page manual, half of which is actually a small coloring book. Includes suggestions for additional activities, as well as a brief glossary, bibliography, and six dinosaur stickers.
Price: Commodore, $34.95; Apple, $39.95

Synopsis: There are five games ranging from simple to complex. They involve counting dinosaurs, or matching a dinosaur with its twin, its food (plant or meat), its natural habitat (air, land, or sea), or its name.

The games use only the arrow and RETURN keys and give musical, animated rewards for correct answers; no response at all for incorrect answers.

Matching a dinosaur to its food is largely a guessing game because 2½ to 5-year-olds have no idea what Ichthyosaurus and Stegosaurus eat. Neither do most 6- to 106-year-olds! When a large, winged creature flew across the screen, I asked Max, "What does he eat?"

"I don't know," he said. "Maybe bird seed."

Matching a dinosaur name to its picture is much too difficult for beginning readers. To make matters worse, the manual lists one beast as Pteranodon while the screen refers to it as a Pternadon. These games require adult supervision.

Manufacturer: ARTWORX SOFTWARE COMPANY, INC.
Address: 150 North Main Street, Fairport, NY 14450
Telephone: 716-425-2833   800-828-6573
Warranty Policy: Free replacement within 90 days of purchase. A $5.00 replacement charge thereafter.

Program Name: HODGE PODGE
THE PLAYFUL ALPHABET
Hardware: Versions for Apple, Atari, Commodore, and IBM.
Suggested Ages: 18 months to 6 years
Documentation: 3-page flyer.
Price: $19.95

Synopsis: An alphabet-awareness game with low-resolution graphics. Pressing any key produces a visual or musical representation of something whose name relates to that key. Type G and view a Goat. Type O and hear *Oh, Susannah!*. Press Q and watch a worm demonstrate the difference between Quick and Slow.

Manufacturer: CBS SOFTWARE
Address: One Fawcett Place, Greenwich, CT 06836
Telephone: 203-622-2525   203-622-2673
Warranty Policy: 90-day warranty covers free replacement "provided that the returned media have not been subjected to abuse, unreasonable use, mistreatment, neglect, or excessive wear;" $5.00 fee after 90 days.

Program Name: ASTRO-GROVER
Hardware: Versions for Apple, Commodore, Atari, and IBM PCjr (optional use of Muppet Learning Keys).
Suggested Ages: 3 to 6
Documentation: Simple, colorful 24-page "Game Play & Activity Manual," including a storybook called *The Zips From Zap.*
Price: Apple and IBM, $19.95; Atari and Commodore, $14.95

Synopsis: ASTRO-GROVER is an early learner's number skills program with excellent sound (especially via the Commodore) and graphics. You help Grover to count Zips from the planet Zap. Five levels progress from easy counting and matching to addition and subtraction. The program provides hints after incorrect responses. Correct answers help Grover to build a beautiful city or to launch a spaceship. An accompanying vinyl keyboard overlay, called EasyKey, fits the contour of the keyboard and makes it easy to find the right key. It effectively covers up all the keys except the numerals and several other keys that the program uses.

CAUTION: Some small fries may want to pick up and examine the overlay or simply remove it from "their" keyboard.

NOTE: ASTRO-GROVER and the following programs featuring the Sesame Street characters were developed for CBS SOFTWARE by the Children's Television Workshop Software Group.

☐ *Program Name:* BIG BIRD'S FUNHOUSE
Hardware: Versions for Atari and Commodore.
Suggested Ages: 3 to 6
Documentation: 24-page, colorfully-illustrated "Game Play & Activity Manual."
Price: $14.95

Synopsis: A clever game of electronic hide and seek. You can invite Muppet friends to play in the elaborate Funhouse, send them scurrying by pressing the HIDE key, then help Big Bird remember where they (as many as 8) are hiding. Clues are given after incorrect guesses; for example, Big Bird shakes his head "No." There are five different levels that progress from simply guessing *which* Muppets are hiding, to *where* they are hiding, to remembering which were invited and *in what order.* There is wonderful music and graphics. The program comes with vinyl EasyKey overlay, featuring pictures of Oscar, Ernie, The Count, etc., positioned over the appropriate keys the child must strike.

☐ *Program Name:* BIG BIRD'S SPECIAL DELIVERY
Hardware: Versions for Atari, Commodore, and IBM.
Suggested Ages: 3 to 6
Documentation: 8-page, illustrated "Game Play & Activity Manual."
Price: $24.95

Synopsis: An "object recognition game." You must help Big Bird and Little Bird to deliver Sesame Street mail by classifying objects (packages). In THE SAME GAME, the child must look at an object and compare it to four others pictured above four storekeepers. The arrow keys are used to move Little Bird to the store with the matching picture. If you were incorrect, the storekeeper will shake his head.

In FIND THE RIGHT KIND, the objects are similar in class or function. For example, a banana goes to the store with the picture of an apple because they are both foods. A drum goes to the store with the trumpet, since they are both musical instruments. There are two levels of difficulty, and bright graphics.

☐ *Program Name:* DR. SEUSS FIX-UP THE MIX-UP PUZZLER

Hardware: Versions for Apple, Atari, and Commodore; optional use of joystick or Muppet Learning Keys.

Suggested Ages: 4 and up

Documentation: 10-page illustrated manual.

Price: Apple, $19.95; Commodore and Atari, $14.95

Synopsis: An electronic jigsaw puzzle featuring six Dr. Seuss characters (including the Cat in the Hat and the Grinch). Children view a puzzle with three Dr. Seuss characters. The computer randomly mixes up the puzzle pieces (at Difficulty Level One, each character becomes separated into head, torso, and feet) and children use simple inputs to reassemble them. Levels Two through Five divide the characters into smaller pieces (some may even be rotated 180 degrees) and pit the child against a built-in timer. These games appear too difficult for many pre-schoolers. (Beyond Level One, Sarah says they all look like "Santa Closet.")

☐ *Program Name:* DUCKS AHOY!

Hardware: Versions for Atari and Commodore (requires a joystick).

Suggested Ages: 3 to 6

Documentation: Comes with 6-page "Game Play Manual" and *Ducks Ahoy!* ("a book of silly duck stuff," including *The Duck Story, The Duck Song,* riddles, and craft activities).

Price: $12.95

Synopsis: Players must guide their gondolas through the canals of Venice, pick up ducks while avoiding a mischievous, often submerged hippo, and drop them off at a nearby beach. Boats can be capsized at any time by the hippo, or by overcrowding (there is a limit of two ducks per boat). After ten ducks are delivered to the beach, they sing their duck song. Players are "encouraged to think logically, helping them develop their abilities to plan ahead." There are very nice graphics, music, and "quacking" sound effects.

☐ *Program Name:* MANY WAYS TO SAY I LOVE YOU
Hardware: Versions for Apple and Commodore.
Suggested Ages: 4 and up
Documentation: Clear, illustrated 16-page booklet.
Price: Apple, $19.95; Commodore, $14.95

Synopsis: An electronic greeting card maker direct from "Mr. Rogers' Neighborhood." The child chooses borders, stickers (graphics), music (including *Won't You Be My Neighbor?*), and words (I LOVE YOU, etc.) to create an on-screen message for someone special. Tots need help with the program and your work cannot be printed, but the creating and sharing of the masterpieces are well worth the effort. *A Family Computing* reviewer referred to the program as "love-processing software." Greeting cards can be saved on disk for later "delivery." The musical, electronic expressions of love are even animated.

I've never understood Mr. Rogers' long-running appeal for children (he's put me to sleep in each of his eighteen years on TV—I call him "Mr. Sominex"), but his warm, smiling face on the cover of this clever software package is a magnet to children. Every time my friend Danielle sees the software, she shrieks with joy, "Mr. Neighborhood! Mr. Neighborhood!"

Manufacturer: KRELL SOFTWARE CORP.
Address: Flowerfield Bldg #7, Suite 1D, St. James, NY 11780
Telephone: 516-584-7900
Warranty Policy: 30-day free disk replacement; a $21.00 charge thereafter.
(KINDERLOGO is also distributed through Educational Computer Services, Inc., P.O. Box 661, Merrimack, NH 03054.)

☐ *Program Name:* KINDERLOGO
Hardware: Apple (KINDERLOGO consists of a disk and manual but needs KRELL or TERRAPIN LOGO as well). A printer is recommended.
Suggested Ages: 3 to 8
Documentation: 141-page manual that emphasizes activities "at and away from the keyboard;" 12 useful appendices.
Price: KINDERLOGO purchased separately, $49.95; together with KRELL'S LOGO, $129.95

Synopsis: A version of the much-acclaimed language, LOGO, scaled down to "small fry size." Commands to direct the LOGO turtle around the screen are reduced to single keystrokes (F for Forward, L for Left turn, C for Circle). Five levels feature two learning games that give children increasing control over the turtle, until they "graduate" to regular LOGO. Designed and created by New Hampshire's Micro-School director, Dorothy Fitch, and first-grade teacher, Priscilla Flanagan, this is the ideal introduction to the ideal first computer language for children.

Children will need help reading the manual and learning the commands at each level. As competence develops, however, they can work creatively with little help from adults. Parents need no previous knowledge of programming to accompany their children through this fascinating world of turtle graphics.

Manufacturer: THE LEARNING COMPANY
Address: 545 Middlefield Road, Menlo Park, CA 94025
Telephone: 415-328-5410, 800-852-2255, (in CA) 800-852-2256
Warranty Policy: Unconditional lifetime guarantee if product is defective or user-damaged. Small duplicating and handling fee.

NOTE: Preview policy within 30 days of purchase—if not satisfied with program, return it along with proof of purchase. You may exchange it for any other LEARNING COMPANY program.

☐ *Program Name:* BUMBLE GAMES
Hardware: Versions for Apple, Atari, Commodore, and IBM (available only through IBM).
Suggested Ages: 4 to 10

Documentation: Brief (24 pages), clear manual, including a glossary and suggestions for additional learning activities away from the computer.
Price: $39.95

Synopsis: An interesting program with six progressively more difficult activities that introduce such concepts as "greater than," "less than," number lines, ordered pairs, and plotting coordinates. Most of the activities are suited for school-age children, but are too advanced for the "day-care" set.

Program Name: GERTRUDE'S SECRETS
Hardware: Versions for Apple, Commodore, and IBM; joystick is optional.
Suggested Ages: 4 to 10
Documentation: Brief (29 pages), clear, illustrated manual, including a map of Gertrude's World, a glossary, and suggestions for additional learning activities away from the computer.
Price: $44.95

Synopsis: GERTRUDE'S SECRETS is an analytical thinking game best suited for the middle and upper range of the 4 to 10 suggested age group. It is filled with puzzles, mazes, colors, and shapes. Gertrude is a puzzle-loving goose whose activities help to develop children's thinking skills (reasoning, inferring patterns and rules, discriminating between similarities and differences).

Children release Gertrude in any puzzle room and she flies away, returning with the pieces of a puzzle. A simple puzzle involves guessing which pieces belong in a box (blue, orange, green, or purple triangles, diamonds, and squares). Perhaps only squares are allowed, or just blue triangles. The child positions a piece in the box. If it stays put—it belongs. If it drops to the bottom of the screen—it doesn't. The child solves the puzzle through trial-and-error. These games are ideal for cooperative play with several children. Use of a joystick is recommended, since keyboard control is too difficult for most preschoolers.

☐ *Program Name:* JUGGLES' RAINBOW
Hardware: Versions for Apple, Atari, Commodore, and IBM.
Suggested Ages: 3 to 6
Documentation: Brief (24 pages), clear, illustrated manual, including suggestions for additional learning activities away from the computer.
Price: $29.95

Synopsis: JUGGLES' RAINBOW includes three games. JUGGLES' RAINBOW teaches the concepts of "above" and "below;" JUGGLES' BUTTERFLY teaches left and right; and JUGGLES' WINDMILL is a combination of the above two games—like above/left or below/right.

☐ *Program Name:* READER RABBIT AND
THE FABULOUS WORD FACTORY
Hardware: Versions for Apple, Atari, Commodore, and IBM; joystick, KoalaPad, or Muppet Learning Keys are optional.
Suggested Ages: 5 to 7
Documentation: 37-page, clear, illustrated manual, including suggestions for additional learning activities away from the computer.
Price: $39.95

Synopsis: Teaches reading skills to tots, utilizing 214 three-letter words. Programs include SORTER, which allows children to sort words according to a "target pattern" (for example, words starting with the letter T). Words travel through the "sorter machine;" children tap the space bar if a match is made, thus placing the word on an appropriate shelf, and do nothing if no match is made (causing the word to fall into a trash barrel below). Speed and choice of target patterns can be selected by parents.

LABELER challenges a child to label shipping cartons. There are three cartons, each with a picture signifying its contents. Below them are three boxes containing three letters each. The first box holds the first letters of each label, the second box holds the second letters, the last box holds the third letters. The child uses simple input commands to unscramble the words.

WORD TRAIN asks the user to fill the train with words from the Word Factory trucks. Each of three trucks displays a three-letter word. The train's locomotive also contains one three-letter word. Using one or two keystrokes, the child adds words to the train. The child must choose words that differ *by one letter* from the last word added to the train.

MATCHUP is a memory game with six different levels of difficulty. The child must point to cards on the screen and press the space bar to turn the card over to see its picture or word. The idea is to match up the various pictures, words, or word parts.

Manufacturer: MINDSCAPE, INC.
Address: 3444 Dundee Road, Northbrook, IL 60062
Telephone: 800-221-9884, (in IL) 800-942-7315
Warranty Policy: 90-day free replacement "provided that the returned media have not been subjected to misuse, damage, or excessive wear."

Program Name: TINKA'S MAZES
Hardware: Versions for Apple, Atari, Commodore, and IBM (joystick is optional).
Suggested Ages: 4 to 8
Documentation: Clear, illustrated 24-page booklet, including suggestions for "Off-Screen Activities."
Price: Apple and IBM, $29.95; Atari and Commodore, $24.95

Synopsis: The SPROUT series of pre-school software from MINDSCAPE is the creation of award-winning children's author and illustrator, Mercer Mayer. Accompany the lovable TinkTonks through interactive adventures (the user chooses options for the robot-like Tinktonks). Most pre-schoolers require adult help reading menus and playing some games (keyboard control of objects is difficult for the smallest fries). The child guides Tinka through mazes laden with math problems. She must get to school, where she can practice Math or go on field trips (and practice Math). There are four levels of difficulty, including lessons on "more or less," counting, and addition. Many lessons are more suitable for school-age children—it is a good package to "grow into."

☐ *Program Name:* TINK'S ADVENTURE
Hardware: Versions for Apple, Atari, Commodore, and IBM.
Suggested Ages: 4 to 8
Documentation: Clear, illustrated 16-page booklet.
Price: Apple and IBM, $29.95; Atari and Commodore, $24.95

Synopsis: TINK'S ADVENTURE features alphabet order and keyboard-familiarity programs with several levels of difficulty. There is optional music and interesting graphics, but Tink's meanderings betray the lack of a story line.

☐ *Program Name:* TINK'S SUBTRACTION FAIR
Hardware: Versions for Apple, Atari, Commodore, and IBM (joystick is recommended).
Suggested Ages: 4 to 8
Documentation: Nicely done, 27-page, illustrated booklet featuring suggestions for "Off-Screen Activities."
Price: Apple and IBM, $29.95; Atari and Commodore, $24.95

Synopsis: Using a joystick or keyboard (a bit awkward), you must pilot Tink throughout the Subtraction Fair, where you can help him to win prizes. Prizes consist of "beepers" and "tonkers" that can be used to pay Tink's fare for playing games (Ring the Bell, Dunk Gork, etc.). There are three levels of difficulty stressing math, memory, and concentration skills. Original music creates a carnival atmosphere. Throughout the SPROUT series, the music often plays when the character stops moving, waiting for the child to make a decision for him. This often makes the children halt Tink in his tracks in order to enjoy the melodies.

☐ *Program Name:* TONK IN THE LAND
OF BUDDY-BOTS
Hardware: Versions for Apple, Atari, Commodore, and IBM (joystick is optional).

Suggested Ages: 4 to 8
Documentation: Clear, illustrated 24-page booklet, with suggestions for "Off-Screen Activities."
Price: Apple and IBM, $29.95; Atari and Commodore, $24.95

Synopsis: The Buddy-Bots need Tonk to collect their parts (scattered all over Buddy-Bot Land) and reassemble them. Choose from four levels of difficulty (Buddy-Bots separated into more parts means more obstacles for you and Tonk to overcome) and play games during your search to win Buddy-Bot parts. Games stress pattern recognition and visual memory skills. They are tough for the youngest small fries.

☐ *Program Name:* TUK GOES TO TOWN
Hardware: Versions for Apple, Atari, Commodore, and IBM.
Suggested Ages: 4 to 8
Documentation: Clear, illustrated 20-page booklet, including suggestions for "Off-Screen Activities."
Price: Apple and IBM, $29.95; Atari and Commodore, $24.95

Synopsis: The child must take Tuk to town, choosing one of eight modes of transportation (Car, Truck, Bus, Train, Motorcycle, Tugboat, Speedboat, Raft) and two of four destinations (Farm, Fair, Forest, Seashore). They stop along the way to play games that teach spelling, vocabulary, and memory skills. Small fries also love the accompanying music.

Manufacturer: RANDOM HOUSE SOFTWARE
Address: Random House Electronic Publishing, 201 East 50th Street, New York, NY 10022
Telephone: 212-751-2600, 800-638-6460 (in MD), 800-492-0782
Warranty Policy: Free repair or replacement of disk within 90 days. For the nine months following the initial 90-day warranty period, defective disks will be replaced *once* for a $5.00 fee.

Program Name: CHARLIE BROWN'S ABC'S
Hardware: Versions for Apple, Commodore, and IBM PCjr with BASIC language cartridge.
Suggested Ages: 3 to 7
Documentation: Nicely done, 28-page manual, including some full-page illustrations of the Peanuts gang. Approximately half of the manual offers suggestions for using the enclosed Activity Cards.
Price: Apple and IBM, $29.95; Commodore, $19.95

Synopsis: Excellent high-resolution graphics and animation make this two-sided program a real treat. The letters A through M are on one disk side, N through Z on the other. Children can view letters in alphabetical or random order. Press a keyboard letter and it will appear on the screen with a Peanuts character. Type the letter again and you can watch and listen to a delightful animated musical sequence. Press the right arrow and see the next letter of the alphabet; press the left arrow and see the previous letter.

The Activity Cards (two sets of 26 small, two-sided cards, and a larger keyboard representation) contain pictures and upper- and lower-case letters that help children to learn the alphabet and its placement on the keyboard.

 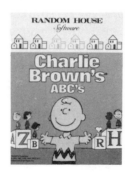

Program Name: PEANUTS MAZE MARATHON
Hardware: Versions for Apple, Commodore, and IBM PCjr with BASIC language cartridge; optional use of joystick.

Suggested Ages: 4 to 8
Documentation: Easy-to-read 12-page, illustrated manual.
Price: Apple and IBM, $29.95; Commodore, $19.95

Synopsis: A maze game that helps to develop eye-hand coordination, left-to-right orientation, and logic skills. The disk is two-sided, with Side One containing simpler mazes than Side Two. The program is a little slow to load and children may become restless while waiting. Those who can read can amuse themselves with on-screen, while-you-wait "fillers," like "Did you know? Your skin weighs twice as much as your brain."

The graphics, though nicely done, are not as endearing as those in CHARLIE BROWN'S ABCs. Computer maze games in general seem to give pre-schoolers trouble. They have difficulty trying to deal with solving the maze while learning the keyboard or joystick controls.

Manufacturer: THE SCARBOROUGH SYSTEM
Address: 55 South Broadway, Tarrytown, NY 10591
Telephone: 914-332-4545
Warranty Policy: Free disk replacement within 30 days; a $5.00 charge thereafter.

Program Name: BUILD A BOOK ABOUT YOU
Hardware: Versions for Apple, Commodore, and IBM (all versions require a printer).
Suggested Ages: 2 to 12
Documentation: 39-page clear, illustrated instruction manual.
Price: $24.95

Synopsis: BUILD A BOOK ABOUT YOU contains everything you need to create, print out, and bind two personalized 8½" × 11" children's storybooks. This delightful program creates 32 full-color, illustrated pages that are then bound in a washable hard cover. This is definitely a family project, as small fries need help with reading instructions, typing in answers to various questions ("What's your name? Your best friend's name?"), printing out the book pages, and binding the finished product (plastic binding strip, needle and string, as well as very clear directions, are provided). The program works with a wide variety of printers. Materials for additional books are sold separately.

When my young friend Bret and his mom created *The Holiday Dragon*, Bret was delighted to learn that a dragon was coming to visit him at 36 Heritage Hill Road in Windham, New Hampshire. And how did the dragon know that Bret's friends' names were Chad, Jason, and Casey? Enthralled with the tale, Bret kept running to the door to see if the dragon had arrived. He even telephoned his friends to spread the news about his soon-to-arrive guest.

Manufacturer: THE SPINNAKER
SOFTWARE CORPORATION
Address: 1 Kendall Square, Cambridge, MA 02139
Telephone: 617-494-1200
Warranty Policy: Free disk replacement during the first 30 days; a $5.00 replacement charge if the disk is physically damaged.

Program Name: ALPHABET ZOO
Hardware: Versions for Apple, Atari, Commodore, and IBM. Optional use of joystick.
Suggested Ages: 3 to 8
Documentation: Brief (9 pages), clear, illustrated manual.
Price: $26.95

Synopsis: ALPHABET ZOO contains an alphabet-awareness game (ABC TIME) and two maze games (THE LETTER GAME and THE SPELLING ZOO). ABC TIME displays the letters of the alphabet in order (showing both upper- and lower-case letters). Along with the letters are graphics of objects whose names begin with the corresponding letters. Every time the program is run, kids see one of several sets of graphics. Thus, one time H will produce a Horse and another time a Hat. Children can either type the first letter of the object's name or tap the space bar to go on to the next letter. Children enjoy this program except for the fact that some of the graphics are difficult to discern (they are somewhat crude, low-resolution graphics).

Color monitors help to make the graphics clearer, but some are still too obscure to recognize.

The maze games require some tricky keyboard manipulation. Even with the optional joystick, children often have difficulty and become somewhat frustrated. The idea of THE LETTER GAME is to move your player around the maze to capture object letters. If a picture of a Zebra is displayed, then you must capture all the Zs in the maze.

In THE SPELLING ZOO, you need to snare entire words one letter at a time. The maze games allow you to choose from six levels of difficulty. Even at the easiest levels, moving around the maze proved to be too difficult for the toddlers I worked with. These are probably better suited for the older members of that 3 to 8 age group.

Program Name: FACEMAKER
Hardware: Versions for Apple, Atari, Commodore, and IBM.
Suggested Ages: 3 to 8
Documentation: Brief (6 pages), clear, illustrated manual.
Price: $24.95

Synopsis: FACEMAKER allows children to construct a variety of faces and animate them (make their eyes wink, ears wiggle, etc.). The program is actually a simple introduction to programming, as the order of facial movements is determined by the child's instructions. FACEMAKER also features a memory game, where the child has to repeat a sequence of moves chosen by the computer. FACEMAKER options, then, are BUILD A FACE, ANIMATE A FACE, and PLAY THE MEMORY GAME. Building a face requires use of just the space bar and the return key. These allow the user to view different eyes, noses, etc., selecting any desired combination. To animate, the user types W for Wink, F for Frown, S for Smile, C for Cry, T to stick out its Tongue, E to wiggle its Ears, and - for a short delay. These *commands* can be written into a *program* that will not be executed until you press RETURN.

Program Name: GRANDMA'S HOUSE
Hardware: Versions for Apple, Atari, and Commodore. Requires a joystick or mouse.
Suggested Ages: 4 to 8
Documentation: Brief (10 pages), clear, illustrated manual.
Price: $24.95

Synopsis: A simple game that allows a child to control characters in search of objects to decorate Grandma's house. Characters can explore a jungle, garden, city, park, beach, furniture store, and appliance store. None of these faraway places is very appealing without a color monitor. Optional music plays only while the characters are not moving. GRANDMA's HOUSE didn't have much "staying power" with the children I worked with. It was very good, however, for acquainting children with the basic controlling movements of the joystick and mouse.

Program Name: KIDS ON KEYS
Hardware: Versions for Apple, Atari, Commodore, and IBM. Joystick is required if the user wants to create graphics to be included in the program.
Suggested Ages: 3 to 9
Documentation: Brief (16 pages), clear, illustrated manual.
Price: $26.95

Synopsis: A computer keyboard familiarity program for small fries. As letters float down the screen, the child must type the matching keys before the letters disappear. There are some variations of this game (pictures whose names must be typed float down the screen) and various levels of difficulty (letters/objects that move faster). The program is a bit difficult for pre-schoolers. School children, however, could use KIDS ON KEYS to learn to touch type.

☐ *Program Name:* KINDER COMP
Hardware: Versions for Apple, Atari, Commodore, and IBM. Joystick is optional.
Suggested Ages: 3 to 8
Documentation: Brief (10 pages), clear, illustrated manual.
Price: $26.95

Synopsis: KINDER COMP features six activities. DRAW enables you to make colorful drawings via the keyboard or joystick; SCRIBBLE repeats a full line of any key that is struck; NAMES asks you to type in your name and then produces scores of that name animated in a sound and light show; SEQUENCE produces five numbers in numerical order and the user must input the next numeral; LETTERS asks the user to press the key that matches the lower case letter displayed on the screen; and MATCH is a pattern-matching game.

DRAW is most popular with the toddler set. Children manipulate the joystick in order to draw and, when things don't come out quite the way they expected, they use their imaginations to decide what it is they *have* drawn. This "draw first, interpret later" style is a great imagination-stretching exercise.

SCRIBBLE and NAMES are also big hits with pre-schoolers and toddlers.

Manufacturer: SPRINGBOARD SOFTWARE, INC.
Address: 7808 Creekridge Circle, Minneapolis, MN 55435
Telephone: 612-944-3915
Warranty Policy: Free disk replacement within 30 days after purchase; a $5.00 charge thereafter. Money-back guarantee if not satisfied with software package.

☐ *Program Name:* EARLY GAMES FOR YOUNG CHILDREN
Hardware: Versions for Apple, Commodore, IBM, and Macintosh.
Suggested Ages: 2½ to 6
Documentation: Clear, 28-page booklet including numerous suggestions for "Activities to Extend Learning On and Off the Computer."
Price: $34.95

Synopsis: Nine nicely-paced games: MATCH NUMBERS, COUNT, ADD, SUBTRACT, MATCH LETTERS, ALPHABET, NAMES, COMPARE SHAPES, and PICTURE DRAW. Graphic letters and numerals are large and colorful, and programs provide clever responses to a child's incorrect answers (see Chapter 3). Games are designed so that children need little adult supervision (menus are in the form of pictures—no reading is necessary). Letter and word games use upper-case letters only. Lively sound effects include a perfectly-choreographed rendition of *Now I Know My ABC's.*

☐ *Program Name:* EASY AS ABC
Hardware: Versions for Apple, Commodore, IBM, and Macintosh.
Suggested Ages: 3 to 6
Documentation: Well-written, 24-page booklet containing the reason for each game, as well as suggestions for additional learning activities away from the computer.
Price: $39.95

Synopsis: Five delightful, colorfully-animated learning games: MATCH LETTERS; electronic DOT-TO-DOT (connect dots alphabetically); HONEY HUNT (help a friendly bee make honey by matching upper- and lower-case letters); LEAPFROG (feed the frogs by indicating which letter comes alphabetically between two others); and LUNAR LETTERS (determine the correct alphabetical sequence of 6 letters). Several of the games provide hints after incorrect responses and most feature full-color graphics as rewards for correct answers. Keyboard controls (arrow keys or the diamond I,J,K,M configuration for up, left, right, and down) take some getting used to, but the results are well worth it.

Program Name: MAKE A MATCH
Hardware: Versions for Apple, Commodore, and IBM.
Suggested Ages: 2½ to 6
Documentation: Clear, 21-page booklet with suggestions for additional learning activities away from the computer.
Price: $29.95

Synopsis: Four learning games (MATCH BY COLOR, MATCH BY SHAPE, GROUP BY SHAPE, and GROUP BY SIZE), each with from four to twelve levels of difficulty. Children develop discrimination skills as they play simple games to match shapes, colors, and sizes. The user can press any key whenever a match is made by the computer. Incorrect responses produce a razzing sound, and on some levels, continued incorrect responses return the program to an easier level. Speed can be set at an agonizingly slow pace. All things considered, this is a well-done but uninspiring program that children seem to get tired of rather quickly.

Program Name: MASK PARADE
Hardware: Versions for Apple and IBM (dot matrix printer required). Joystick is optional.
Suggested Ages: 4 to 12
Documentation: Well-done, 29-page, illustrated booklet containing suggestions for additional learning activities away from the computer.
Price: $39.95

Synopsis: You can create, print out, color, cut out, and *wear* masks, hats, badges, glasses, jewelry, ties, and other items. This exciting program uses simple picture menus and icons (Mom and Dad need to help pre-schoolers with the program and in handling scissors carefully—such working together is one of the wonderful advantages of the software). Simple keyboard or joystick controls are used to make masks by selecting icons for facial outline, eyes, nose, and mouth. Then you can make changes in your masterpiece or create your own from scratch by selecting the crayon icon.

MASK PARADE is terrific for role-playing, imagination-stretching, and just plain fun! The jewelry and hats are perfect for "getting into" a part for dramatic play. Be careful, though—some tots are frightened by masks.

Bethy left Cammie's Day Care one day wearing her "hot off the press" chef's hat and the two were inseparable for hours. She wore it shopping, to a restaurant—even in the pouring rain!

If you can buy only one piece of software to use with your pre-schooler, this is the one to get. Extra nice results can be obtained by using heavy bond colored computer stationery and colored ribbons (supplied by PIXELLITE COMPUTER PROD-UCTS, INC., 5221 Central Ave., Suite 205, Richmond, CA 94804, Telephone: 800-643-0800).

Program Name: RAINBOW PAINTER
Hardware: Versions for Apple and Commodore (joystick or KoalaPad is optional).
Suggested Ages: 4 and up
Documentation: Clear, illustrated 19-page booklet.
Price: $34.95

Synopsis: This is computer artwork at its most colorful. The program requires adult supervision to help small fries learn to manipulate the picture menus via keyboard, joystick, or KoalaPad (menus and icons are similar to MASK PARADE). Although this is a powerful drawing program for older children, pre-schoolers love to simply select a color (by pointing the cursor to it and pressing a joystick or KoalaPad button or space bar) and fill in an area of their picture with that color (by moving the cursor into position and tapping the appropriate button or space bar again). What fun! There are 50 pictures and 110 colors and patterns provided on the disk. Altering pictures or creating them from scratch requires finer motor skills than most pre-schoolers possess, but the above-mentioned coloring activity is very satisfying for such youngsters. The pictures that come with the program include sketches of animals, vehicles, space, dinosaurs, and fairy tales. Icons are quite clever—you point to a paint can to select different color sets, to a disk to save or load a picture, to a trash barrel to discard the drawing altogether.

RAINBOW PAINTER is a "coloring book on a disk," with some very creative artistic tools and activities. Small fries can grow along with this package.

Manufacturer: WEEKLY READER FAMILY SOFTWARE
Address: Field Publications, 245 Long Hill Road, Middletown, CT 06457
Telephone: 203-638-2571
Warranty Policy: Free repair or replacement of defective disk within 30 days of purchase.

Program Name: STICKYBEAR ABC
Hardware: Versions for Apple, Atari, and Commodore.
Suggested Ages: 3 to 6
Documentation: Brief instruction guide—the only directions necessary ("Press any letter") are on-screen. The program comes with a colorful poster. The Atari and Apple versions come with a hardcover, illustrated storybook and a set of stickers.
Price: Apple, $39.95; Atari and Commodore, $29.95

Synopsis: An entertaining alphabet- and keyboard-awareness program that requires little adult supervision. It is similar to ALPHABET ZOO's ABC TIME, but has much better graphics and animation to boot. There are two musical, high-resolution graphic illustrations for each letter of the alphabet. Illustrations are well-chosen for a young audience—Umbrella and Underwear for U, Zebra and Zipper for Z. STICKYBEAR characters are also quite lovable.

The hardcover book is a picture- and word-recognition tool showing familiar objects in a toy store, supermarket, home, etc.

☐ *Program Name:* STICKYBEAR NUMBERS
Hardware: Apple, Atari, Commodore, and IBM.
Suggested Ages: 3 to 6
Documentation: 4-page flyer containing simple instructions and suggestions for additional learning activities away from the computer.
Price: Apple and IBM, $39.95; Atari and Commodore, $29.95

Synopsis: A well-done counting- and number-recognition program, similar in format to STICKYBEAR ABC. Pressing a number causes that many objects to appear (trains, birds, snowmen, etc.). The program is nicely animated, and comes with stickers, a hardcover book, and a color poster. Commodore comes without stickers and storybook.

☐ *Program Name:* STICKYBEAR OPPOSITES
Hardware: Apple, Atari, and Commodore, with optional use of mouse or paddles.
Suggested Ages: 3 to 6
Documentation: 4-page flyer containing directions and suggestions for additional learning activities away from the computer.
Price: Apple, $39.95; Atari and Commodore, $29.95

Synopsis: This is another fun program in the STICKYBEAR series. This one teaches opposites (happy-sad, fast-slow, above-below) in an entertaining way. Left and right arrow keys alternate the animation; for example, press one and the airplane flies below the bridge—press the other and it flies above. The space bar advances the program to the next word pair (there are 21 word pairs in all). Apple and Atari include stickers and storybook.

☐ *Program Name:* STICKYBEAR SHAPES
Hardware: Apple, Atari, and Commodore, with optional use of mouse or paddles.
Suggested Ages: 3 to 6
Documentation: 4-page flyer containing directions and suggestions for additional learning activities away from the computer.
Price: Apple, $39.95; Atari and Commodore, $29.95

Synopsis: Yet another entertaining STICKYBEAR package designed to help children to identify circles, squares, triangles, rectangles, and diamonds. It consists of three games. PICK IT requires children to identify the missing shape in a picture. NAME IT lets children match shapes with their names, and FIND IT asks them to match a sample shape with one hidden in the picture. The program requires simple input using a keyboard, mouse, or paddles. Apple and Atari versions, too, come with stickers and a hardcover book.

OTHER USEFUL PROGRAMS NOT TARGETED SPECIFICALLY FOR PRE-SCHOOLERS

There are numerous other programs, including art and music packages designed for adults or older children, that many parents use with their pre-school children. DAZZLE DRAW by BRODERBUND, BANK STREET MUSIC WRITER and BANK STREET STORY BOOK by MINDSCAPE, and SONG-WRITER by THE SCARBOROUGH SYSTEM are examples of excellent programs that can be used in this way. Additional programs are discussed on the following pages.

Manufacturer: BRODERBUND
Address: 17 Paul Drive, San Rafael, CA 94903
Telephone: 415-479-1900
Warranty Policy: Free replacement within 90 days; a $5.00 charge (plus $2.50 for postage and handling) "if disk has been physically damaged," or after 90 days.

Program Name: BANK STREET WRITER
Hardware: Versions for Apple, Atari, Commodore, and IBM (printer is recommended).
Suggested Ages: For writers and would-be writers of all ages
Documentation: Clear, illustrated 28-page manual.
Price: Atari and Commodore, $49.95; Apple, $69.95; IBM, $79.95

Synopsis: Although most pre-schoolers cannot read and write, dictating stories and letters is well within their reach. This friendly word processor, designed for children in conjunction with the Bank Street College of Education, may be just the thing to nurture interest in creative writing. Commands remain in view at the top of the screen, in the "prompt" area—you type below, in the "text" area. Since the commands remain in view, you don't have to remember them. The program includes an excellent tutorial on the flip side of the disk that provides enough documentation even for people with no computer experience. The trade-off for this simplicity, as you might suspect, is in the lack of powerful features (except for the enhanced IBM version). But BANK STREET WRITER should handle most of the family's writing needs—from letters, stories, and poems to book reports and term papers. Other products in this popular series, including BANK STREET SPELLER (a spelling checker) and BANK STREET FILER (a data manager), follow the same, easy-to-use style.

Program Name: THE PRINT SHOP
Hardware: Versions for Apple, Atari, Commodore, and IBM
Suggested Ages: 6 through adult
Documentation: Excellent 27-page, illustrated 8½″ × 11″ reference manual.
Price: Atari and Commodore, $44.95; Apple, $49.95; IBM, $59.95

Synopsis: A wonderful program that lets users create greeting cards, signs, letterheads, and banners. Easy-to-use, on-screen directions are all that's necessary. Small fries need help operating the program and the printer, but they can really produce some great creations. Bret's mom helped him to make a greeting card with hearts, flowers, and the proclamation, "I love Mommy, Daddy, Casey [his brother], Nukato [their Rhodesian Ridgeback], and myself." Users need to know nothing about computer graphics to create professional-looking results. BRODERBUND sells additional GRAPHICS LIBRARY disks for $24.95 each ($34.95 for IBM), as well as heavy bond colored stationery for use with THE PRINT SHOP.

☐ *Program Name:* WELCOME ABOARD—A MUPPET
☐ CRUISE TO COMPUTER LITERACY
   Hardware: Versions for Apple (IIc and IIe only); Commo-
   dore (joystick is optional).
   Suggested Ages: "First-time and novice computer users of
   all ages"
   Documentation: Brief flyer; most documentation is on-
   screen and easy-to-follow (for readers, of course).
   Price: Apple, $39.95; Commodore, $24.95

Synopsis: A great program to introduce school-age children to
the concepts of the five basic computer applications (programming, word processing, computer-aided design, database management, and games). The Muppets are on board (Kermit is
the captain at the bridge, Miss Piggy at the Salon De Beaute,
Fozzie Bear at the Joke Library) to give you tours of the various
rooms. You learn SLOWGO, the Muppets' own version of
LOGO, explore database systems in Fozzie Bear's Joke Library,
and discover word processing in Scooter's Message Center.

   Bethy, a riddle and joke fan from way back, loves Fozzie
Bear's Joke Library. One of her favorite jokes is, "What do you
call a frozen dog?" Answer—"a pupsicle." She learned to do
"key word searches" on the data base, searching for, say, all the
"pickle" jokes. (Speaking of pickles, Sarah began calling a pickle
"a sour cute number," thereby earning the nickname, Sara
Cutenumber. Now, when her father comes to pick her up after
day-care, the other children welcome him as "Mr. Cutenumber.")

MUPPET CRUISE features colorful graphics and comes with a clever 12-page glossary booklet called, *The Muppet Guide To Computerese*. The program is worthwhile for small fries to grow into.

Manufacturer: COMPUTEROSE, INC.
Address: 2012 East Randol Mill Road, Suite 223, Arlington, TX 76011
Telephone: 817-461-1333
Warranty Policy: Free disk replacement within 90 days of purchase.

Program Name: CHILDPACE
Hardware: Versions for Apple, Commodore, and IBM.
Suggested Ages: For use with children 3 to 60 months
Documentation: Clear 27-page, illustrated booklet, including suggested Professional Resources, as well as a "Dear Physician" letter explaining CHILDPACE to the doctor and encouraging his professional diagnosis which ". . . no amount of home testing can replace."
Price: $39.95

Synopsis: A program to help parents assess their children's rate of development (general movement, detailed movement, language, and personal/social skills), comparing it with that of other children the same age. "It is not intended as a substitute for professional consultation." The package contains a program disk and testing materials used by the testers (Mom & Dad) and scorers (also Mom & Dad). The test should be administered every three or four months during the child's first two years, provided that previous test results show no "delay" or "behind schedule" messages. After two years, the test should be administered every six months.

The authors give good, commonsense suggestions concerning interpreting test results, advising parents when and when not to be concerned with "behind schedule" results. CHILDPACE is based on developmental norms "published in the *Journal of Pediatrics* and used in the Denver Developmental

Screening Test." The impressive package allows parents to record the progress of their child's developmental milestones. It is definitely worth a look.

A WORD ABOUT SPEECH SYNTHESIZERS

Speech synthesis (adding voice to your computer) and preschoolers go well together. For one thing, they are about the same age. But even though speech synthesis is still in its infancy, synthesizers are available for most personal computers. Some plug in with interface cards, some are external devices, and most have accompanying software. You should look for a text-to-speech mode, allowing you to type in a word and have the computer say it back. Small fries will clearly get the message that the letters they type at the keyboard are the building blocks of speech.

The one that we joyfully experiment with at Cammie's Day Care is SAM (Software Automatic Mouth). When I first hooked up SAM to our Apple computer, I ran to the day-care play area and excitedly told the children, "Guess what—my computer can talk now!" Amazed, Devony came back with, "It *can*! How old is it?"

SAM speaks in several voices, most of which have a robotic but generally understandable sound. I hooked up our computer speaker to our record player speakers and was able to announce the arrival of parents in stereo. Devony's Uncle Craig is affectionately known as Craiger. But when SAM announced, "Devony, your Uncle Craiger is here," all the children laughed gleefully, asking who it was that had an Uncle Cracker!

SAM is manufactured by TRONIX (8295 S. La Cienaga Boulevard, Inglewood, CA 90301. Telephone: 213-215-0353) and runs on Apple, Atari, and Commodore computers—cost is $59.95 for Atari and Commodore (speech synthesizer entirely on disk); $99.95 for Apple (price includes disk and required interface card). Other popular speech and music synthesizers include ECHO+ from STREET ELECTRONICS (1140 Mark Ave., Carpinteria, CA 93013, $129.00 for Apple; $249.00 for IBM, 805-684-4593), and MOCKINGBOARD from SWEET MICRO SYSTEMS, INC. (50 Freeway Drive, Cranston, RI 02920, $179, 800-341-8001).

8

Computers in Perspective

Admittedly, this has been a whirlwind tour of the computer world for very young children. I've tried to give you a brief outline of what materials are available to you and how you can best make use of them. The rest is up to you. But before we part company I would like to address some more or less random concerns that I often hear from parents.

A COMMONSENSE APPROACH

When first asked to write *Computers and Small Fries*, I balked. I couldn't help thinking of all the computer sales hype, implying that the computer was going to solve all the world's problems—those of education in particular. Computer manufacturers were urging parents to start their children computing at a very early age. And some parents were eating it right up. They were convinced that the computer was the "greatest educational tool since chalk," that their children's futures would be ruined if they didn't get into the fourth grade computer class, and that non-computing kids were destined to be "lost in the technological dust." Most of this was nonsense, of course. The computer would certainly solve some problems, but it would also create others. It might be a great boon to some people, but a useless pile of circuitry to others. The more I thought about writing the book, however, the clearer some things became:

"I'm sorry, honey, but you can't play with your computer
until you finish the game."

- All the hoopla aside, it was obvious that computers *could* be powerful educational tools and *would* indeed be a big part of our children's futures. Therefore . . .

- We parents should help to ease our children into the computing environment, to ensure that computers would have a positive impact on them. And . . .

- Easing kids into that computing environment *might* best be done by starting them early (gently nudging, mind you—not shoving).

We need to approach computing with common sense because the computer revolution is still new. There are no definitive studies yet. No one knows for sure what will happen in the future. "Computer companies and magazines are folding left and right," said one computer hobbyist. "They don't know the future—nobody does." But let's be cautiously optimistic about computers, monitoring our family's experience so that the micro's influence is *not* negative.

BLOCKS, FINGERPAINTS, AND COMPUTERS

The computer is just another medium for children to experience, just as they use blocks, fingerpaints, and story books. The richer and more varied a child's environment, the better.

We must remember, however, that some things are best taught without a computer. To teach a child to read, for example, all you really need is a child, a book, and some time together. But if you want to increase an older child's reading rate, a speed-reading program might come in handy. Another important point to be made is that the computing experience should be *in addition to* other experiences, not *in place of* them. It's neat to manipulate graphics on a screen, but children need to manipulate concrete objects in the real world, too. Children need real world experiences. They need to touch and feel (and, of course, sometimes taste!) crayons and paints, etc. Painting with computer graphics can be quite creative. But making a mess—spilling paints, getting your hands and clothes soiled, feeling the texture of the materials—is a vital learning experience as well. I feel the same way about my own computing experience. Although I enjoy the computer basketball game, LARRY BIRD AND DR. J GO ONE ON ONE, after twenty minutes or so I want to get out there in the driveway with my kids and shoot some *real* hoops.

WON'T COMPUTERS COME BETWEEN PEOPLE?

Only if we let them. An essential point is that computing should be a *family* experience. Whatever computer-related stuff we want to expose our youngsters to (if and when they get interested) should be shared *with* them. I hope we don't turn the kids over to the machine! I envision the child sitting on his parent's lap in front of the computer, as they learn and play together. Such an experience will *bring families together*. But I can also envision a parent who is ready to play a greater role in his child's high school education, and says one Saturday morning, "Okay Susie, it's 9 A.M. Work on this Algebra I software program up in the computer room—I'll see you at lunchtime." An experience like this will *come between families*.

PINK AND BLUE COMPUTERS?

Are girls getting shortchanged in the computer revolution?

So far, boys outnumber girls in computer courses and computer camps. And, of course, video arcades are heavily dominated by males. If we are not careful, our children can easily fall into a computer age sexist trap.

Perhaps boys have greater intrinsic aptitude or interest in computers. But I doubt it. Girls have no less interest or ability—just less experience. Too many of us believe the myth that "girls can't handle the abstract thinking that computer operation requires." Couple this parental attitude with the fact that much software is geared toward what has traditionally been male domain—sports, competition, aggressive/violent games. Magazine ads also picture more males than females playing happily at the keyboard.

Sexist child rearing may be the real culprit in computer inequality of the sexes, however. At gift-giving times, when we give our sons footballs and computers and our daughters "Sally Do-Right Bake Sets," the message that we deliver is pretty obvious!

To keep our daughters from being swallowed up by the sexist trap, we should start them computing early. Research indicates that there are practically no differences in aptitude between toddlers of different sexes. This "starting early" may mean simply letting the toddlers bang away on the keyboard when the spirit moves them. They'll see that the computer is a tool used by all members of the family. It is important, then, for mothers to serve as computing role models. Also, when our children enter school, we should stay in touch with school officials to ensure that our daughters are not steered away from math, science, and computer courses.

WILL COMPUTERS TAKE THE TEACHER'S PLACE?

A good answer, considering some of the teachers I've known, is "I certainly hope so." An equally good answer, considering some of the teachers I've known, is "I certainly hope not." The making of a good teacher has little to do with degrees or credentials, but much to do with human qualities like kindness, a sense of humor, and a genuine love of learning and of children. Keep in mind that computers are just tools. We parents are the teachers. Computers can't replace us in that role—but they can be used well by wise teachers. The computer is the most general, all-purpose teaching tool yet devised by humans. But kind, loving parents won't allow these machines to take their place—instead, they'll use them with love and good humor.

My friend Sean was in the fourth grade when he first realized that the computer couldn't take his teacher's place. He was working late into the night on an entertaining math drill program, called MUSICAL MATH TEACHER. The program drills the user on math facts, rewards correct answers with a brief musical interlude, and keeps a running percentage score. Sean's father entered the room, noted that his son had 499 of 500 problems correct, and asked, "Why are you working so late?"

"Well Dad," Sean answered, "I got one problem wrong earlier and I've worked my score up to 99% correct—and I'm not going to bed till I get all the way back to 100%!"

THE BOTTOM LINE—COMPUTERS AND
SMALL FRIES CAN BE PLAIN FUN

I like pre-schoolers. I like computers. And they seem to go pretty well together. I recall working with Raquel one afternoon and really enjoying her comments and her company. "You're so smart," I said to her.

"I know . . . I don't have a 'puter, though. On Sesame they got a 'puter like you."

"I like you a lot, Raquel."

"I like you, too." Not taking her eyes off the screen, she added, "I like your 'puter."

Appendix
A Computer Station
You Can Build

The computer station pictured above is extremely easy to build. Exhibit A for the defense—I built it—and I am a basket case around power tools, blueprints, and most machines. (The rather distinguished-looking balding gentleman in the photo is me.) Okay, so I had a little help from a neighbor who used to be a furniture maker. He helped with the plans and built the wooden brace that supports the counter in the center. And he helped me to write clear instructions on how to construct the brace.

WHAT'S SO SPECIAL ABOUT THIS SET-UP?

The computer station pictured above:

- is easy to build (follow my step-by-step instructions).

- allows for plenty of desk space to spread out materials (it is ideal for students and grown-ups who need writing space, computing space, and just general "spread-out" space).

- solves the problem of storage of software, books, magazines, manuals, stationery, and keyboard alternatives. Keeping everything in its place affords maximum protection for all your computer belongings. You can use the high shelves for "taboo" items that must be kept out of children's reach. Besides the shelves, which can be positioned to accommodate books of varying sizes, the two large (28 inches deep) file drawers are handy storage devices. A family of four might allot one drawer to each family member. (*Your* family of four might do that—however, I have allotted *myself* all four drawers.)

- allows for great flexibility in arranging your equipment. You can put peripherals to the left, right, or on any of the shelves. I often put my monitor one shelf higher when I give demos (computerese for demonstrations) to our local computer club beginners' group. That way, they can see over my head. Bouncing the light from the adjustable light fixture off the ceiling reduces glare off the screen (and off my scalp).

- is very convenient for parents and children to work/play side-by-side. There are no annoying table legs in the way. Sometimes our children pull the piano bench up to the keyboard and share the seat.

- has a built-in, three-inch space through which computer paper can feed. This three-inch space results from the fact that the file cabinets are 28 inches deep, while the standard counter top that sits on them is 25 inches deep. Don't forget that there are some excellent computer programs that, with your help, allow your pre-school children to create their own printouts. Place a box of computer paper on the floor under the counter (just below the printer). Feed the paper up through the three-inch space and into the printer. Outcoming paper can fall through the same three-inch space and collect neatly (or at least semi-neatly) on the floor until you are ready to retrieve it.

- requires you to give up only one wall—not an entire room—to the computer. This is often a handy solution for families whose homes are already bursting at the seams. When I first mentioned my desire to enter the computer age, even my dear, sweet, calm, unassuming wife, Cammie, asked politely—"A computer? A *computer*?? Where the *&%$## are we going to put the %&$#!$% thing?" A large room might be divided, allowing the computer room to double as a den, study, or library. We did finally give up an entire room to the computer. We sold our living room furniture (it was one of those Italian living rooms, anyway—the ones that look so nice but nobody can ever enter). We added a desk and a bookcase and now the room is fully functional. But I had to promise my wife that the room would soon make me a prolific and successful writer, so please recommend this book to all your friends!

MATERIALS NEEDED

To build the computer station, you will need the materials discussed below:

- **1 standard counter top** (length depends on the length of the wall against which you will place it). The one pictured is 11 feet, 5 inches long. I purchased a standard 12-foot long counter top with splashback (the 4-inch high backing) and my neighbor used a cross-cut saw (a saw with 24 teeth per inch) to cut it. He tells me that a home handyman is more likely to have a router in his workshop. That will do the trick as well, but I suggest getting the building supply house that sells the counter to cut it for you.

- **2 two-drawer files.** I prefer the high sides that allow you to use hanging folders without extra hardware (or else you have to put in metal inserts, called letter size frames, which are available at office supply stores). Again, the files pictured are 28 inches deep. This leaves a 3-inch space when the counter top is placed on the files—ideal for paper feed from below. But you can use file cabinets with different dimensions and adjust the set-up to allow for the paper feed. Since much of the cabinets is actually hidden, you may want to refurbish some inexpensive, used ones. Check flea markets/ yard sales or used office furniture places. Bang out the dents with a hammer, add a little spray paint, and you'll be in business.

- **Several shelves.** The number of shelves depends on your own personal taste and the height of the wall against which you are placing them.

- **Standards.** These are the metal rods that screw into the wall vertically, forming the supporting framework for your shelves. You may want standards long enough to go from ceiling to floor, or just from ceiling to counter-top height. The number that you will need again depends on personal taste and the length of the wall. The studs used for house-framing are usually 16 inches apart, so you might place standards every 16 or 32 inches apart. A lot depends on how much weight the set-up will finally support.

  Several carpenter friends of mine expressed concern over the weight I was placing on the shelves. One thought that I should add more standards. Another thought that I had enough standards, but that I should use longer screws to fasten them to the walls. I used 1½-inch wood screws; he suggested 2-inchers. I chose to do neither, partly because I'm so tired of getting opposing viewpoints from "experts" and partly because I'm too lazy to redo the whole thing. My wife keeps warning me that one day she'll come home and find me buried under an avalanche of books and computer parts. Play it safe—use longer screws and more standards.

- **Brackets.** These are the metallic things that fit into the standards and hold up the shelves. To determine how many brackets you will need, count the number of standards that will be used and multiply this by the number of shelves you want.

- **Screws for standards.** 1½-inch to 2-inch flat head wood screws. To determine how many you will need, count the number of screw holes in each bracket and multiply this by the number of standards.

- **Power strip that allows for 6 or 8 plugs** (and also has holes for attaching to wall or other object). You might consider a power strip that has a built-in "surge suppressor." This protects against unexpected electrical power surges or "spikes" that may damage your hardware.

- **Tools.** The necessary tools are: screw driver, hammer, pencil, electric drill, level, and router or cross-cut saw.

MATERIALS FOR OPTIONAL BRACE

- **One two-by-four** (you will need two pieces, one about 26½ inches long and another approximately 20 inches long).

- **One one-by-two** (you will need two pieces, each about 20 inches long).

- **Screws for brace** (you will need two 2-inch flat head wood screws). Constructing the wooden brace (see diagram) is the most difficult part of the project and it's actually pretty easy.

- **Four 1½-inch flat head wood screws** to fasten one-by-three to brace.

- **Four 2-inch flat head wood screws** to attach brace to wall.

- **Two 2-inch flat head wood screws** to attach brace to counter top.

- **Carpenter's glue** (sometimes called "white glue"—please, no Superglue).

- **Hand saw.**

STEP-BY-STEP INSTRUCTIONS

The following instructions are for the set-up pictured. Use them as a guideline, tailoring them to your room's specifications and your own personal taste. Each step describes the simplest possible method. If you are a genuine handyman, you can add more "polish" to the project. The instructions below are, however, written for "unhandymen" (like me).

Step 1—Fasten standards to wall.

First decide how many standards you want to put up. Check the wall for studs by tapping gently with your knuckles or a hammer (locate the center of the one in either corner—then measure sixteen inches over to the center of each successive stud). Use a level to keep each standard plumb. Mark the spots where screws will go and then use an electric drill to get the holes started. Note that the tops of each standard must line up. If the ceiling is off, you may actually have to put each successive standard a fraction of an inch higher or lower than the preceding one. Use a level to determine this. Also, be aware that the standards have a top and a bottom, and must go in right-side-up. Check their placement before marking spots for holes. Place the standards into position and insert the 1½- or 2-inch flathead wood screws. If all the screws don't find a stud, you can use "toggle bolts." A reversible drill will make things easier (allowing you to screw and unscrew with an electric advantage), but if you can't get one, do what I do. Put a little soap on the threads of the screws and a little elbow grease on the screw driver.

Step 2—Set file cabinets into position.

Align the two file cabinets, one on each side of the wall. Make sure that the drawers will open (for example, they might bump into baseboard heaters). You may want to leave additional space instead of placing them close to the walls. Stand back and have a look.

Step 3—Insert the top-most shelf brackets.

Attach the brackets for the top shelves. It is easier to do this now, before the counter top is in your way. You can get at the bottom ones later. As a matter of fact, attaching the bottom ones now might become a nuisance for you when you are setting the counter top in place. There is a knack to setting the brackets in correctly. I find that if you insert them and then tap down gently at the back of the bracket with a hammer, they will snap into place nicely. If, when you try to place the shelf on them, the slightest jar sends them crashing to the floor, then they haven't snapped into place nicely!

Step 4—Place the top shelves on the brackets.

Again, it's easier to do this before the counter is in place. Shelves should be cut so that their length fits snugly (no more than a quarter-inch less than the actual left-to-right measurement of your wall). In this way, objects won't fall through the space remaining between the shelf edges and walls. Measure each shelf individually, at the height at which it will go, since the wall may not be of uniform length from top to bottom.

The other dimensions of the shelves themselves can vary. I suggest one inch thick by at least 8 inches deep. If you can, get dried stock (kiln dried) so that the wood doesn't bend and warp as moisture evaporates.

Step 5—Set the counter top on the file cabinets.

Cut the counter top about one-quarter of an inch less than the length of the wall against which it will be placed. Be sure to measure the wall length at the height that the counter will finally be placed. You will need help to set the counter in place (one foreman to supervise and two hardhats to handle the bullwork). "There's a happy medium here somewhere, fellas," cautioned my neighbor, the furniture maker, as we bobbed and weaved Laurel and Hardy style. Once set in place, you will be able to judge whether or not you need a brace in the center. (A counter 6 feet long or more probably needs bracing.) Don't let the unit sag in the middle. Don't put any weight on it, and be sure to prop it up somehow while you build the brace.

Step 6—Insert the remaining shelf brackets.

Step 7—Cut and place the remaining shelves into position.

Step 8—Place the power strip into position.

Decide where you can best put the power strip so that it helps to make wires least accessible. You may want to fasten it to the wall or the base of the counter. Set up your computer. You will need one outlet for the computer, one for the monitor, one for the printer, and one for the light fixture.

Step 9—Brace.

Refer to Diagram #1 and build the brace that is pictured there. From the two-by-four cut two pieces (one 26½ inches long and the other 20 inches long). Predrill two holes near the end of the 20-inch piece and partly into the end of the 26½-inch piece. Apply carpenter's glue to the interface of these two pieces and fasten with two 2-inch flat head wood screws. Be sure to keep a right angle between these two pieces.

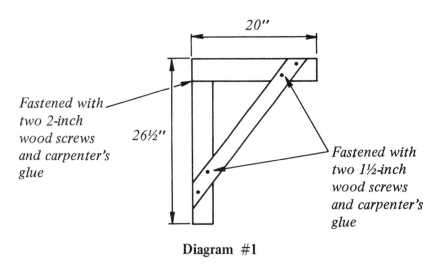

Diagram #1

Position the one-by-two as in Diagram #2. Letting each end overhang as shown, draw a pencil line on the one-by-two to mark where it should be cut. Cut the one-by-three along those lines. Use it as a "template" to cut a second piece of the same length.

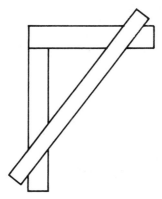

Diagram #2

Using 1½-inch flat head wood screws and carpenter's glue, attach the one-by-two as shown in Diagram #3 (one on each side of the brace).

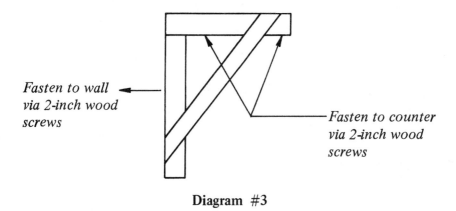

Fasten to wall via 2-inch wood screws

Fasten to counter via 2-inch wood screws

Diagram #3

Position the brace and attach it to the wall and to the counter top with the 2-inch flat head wood screws (be sure not to puncture the counter top—it is usually only ¾-inch thick).

For fastening the brace to the wall you may need screws longer than two inches. This depends on the thickness of the building materials they must pass through before "finding" a stud. Again, if screws do not "find" studs, you can use toggle bolts.

Stand back and have a look. They say that Bill Bradley, when he was playing basketball for the New York Knicks, could tell if the hoop was a quarter of an inch off. Well, pretend you're Bradley. Slam dunk a screwdriver. Make adjustments if necessary. Now fill the shelves up with all the books, magazines, software, computer peripherals, and other junk that by now is probably strewn all over the house. You will find that this involves taking down the brackets and realigning the shelves about thirty-seven times before getting it just right. Computer types refer to this as "reconfiguring the system."

When you're done, be sure to invite the kids in—and have a family celebration!

Index

About the Author

Mario Pagnoni is a computer education teacher and writer. He received his Master in Education from American International College. His many humorous articles and software reviews have appeared in *Byte, Micro, InCider*, and the *Boston Globe*. He has appeared on numerous television and radio talk shows, and continues to lecture and speak about computers and education. He is also the author of *The Complete Home Educator*. He and his family reside in Methuen, Massachusetts.